What Is Heaven Like?

Morton Kelsey

What Is Heaven Like?

The Kingdom as Seen in the Beatitudes

New City Press

Dedication

To my friends
on the other side
of the communion of saints

Published in the United States by New City Press
202 Cardinal Rd., Hyde Park, NY 12538
©1997 Morton Kelsey

Artwork on cover by Ave Center, Loppiano, Italy
Cover design by Nick Cianfarani

Library of Congress Cataloging-in-Publication Data:
Kelsey, Morton T.
    What is heaven like? : the kingdom as seen in the Beatitudes / by
Morton Kelsey.
        p.   cm. — (Today's issues)
    Includes bibliographical references.
    ISBN 1-56548-091-0
        1. Heaven—Christianity—Biblical teaching.   2. Beatitudes-
-Devotional literature.   I. Title. II. Series.
BT382.K45   1997
236'.24—dc21   96-46246
                                                                CIP

1st printing: January 1997
2d printing: November 1997

Printed in the United States of America

Contents

The Good News About Heaven

A streak of lightning can flash across the sky and turn the darkest night into day. In the same way Jesus' message about the kingdom of heaven flashed across Palestine and the Roman empire and brought hope and light to conquered nations and oppressed people. Hope was even given to the slaves — nearly half the population of that empire. Jesus' message was simple and straightforward: "The time has come when your hope can be fulfilled. Heaven, where God rules with tender love, has drawn very close. Change your way of living; give up your fear and hate. Taste the utter joy of the fellowship of God's heaven" (Mk 15:14-15, Mt 4:17, author's paraphrase). This message — this proclamation of good news — was the foundation of Jesus' ministry and his gospel. People of all stations of life flocked to hear this new prophet, whose treatment of people was in tune with his message. Jesus healed the sick, cast out demonic fear, and gave people reason to live again; he renewed people's hope that the Holy One of Israel truly cared for them.

Jesus' ministry, after beginning in Galilee, gradually spread throughout the Roman empire, for God had prepared a fertile field for Jesus' proclamation. Ordinary people lived grim lives in Palestine during the years after Herod's death. Rome had consolidated its control over this conquered people, and Roman legions, placed everywhere in Palestine, maintained a fragile peace. The emperor and his servants found it easier to deal with a few wealthy priestly families, large landlords, and native tax collectors than with a nation of small farmers — and the presence of these wealthy natives also gave Palestine the appearance of a free country. So ordinary peasants were ignored, becoming mere numbers in the imperial register.

The backbone of Jewish society, the modestly successful peasant farmer, simply disappeared during this time, and the fabric of social life disintegrated. Unemployment was rife. Some people waited in village squares to be called to work, while others looked for work desperately, aimlessly wandering through the countryside. Some stooped so low as to feed the pigs of gentile landlords. These people began not to keep the ritual law, which was much stricter than the moral law; these dispossessed who could not follow the law were despised by their religious leaders. Deep despair and hopelessness hung over Israel like a violent storm.

This was the soil that God had prepared for the planting of the message of hope. Men and women were seeking any signal of meaning. A few years before Jesus appeared, John the Baptist began to proclaim his message of hope; he announced that people could repent and ask God for forgiveness. As a sign of their new life, they were baptized in the Jordan River. Thousands upon thousands came from Jerusalem and from all over Palestine to be baptized by John. Many people from all stations of life believed that he was the prophet who could save Israel.

An ordinary carpenter from Nazareth, Jesus by name, was drawn to the Jordan by John's message. He was baptized by John in the Jordan. As he was coming up out of the water, Jesus saw the heavens open, and he heard a voice like thunder speaking: "You are my beloved Son; with you I am well pleased" (Mt 3:17). After this tremendous experience, Jesus went out into the desert to fast and meditate on what his ministry was to be. There he was tempted by the forces of evil, but he withstood the onslaught, and angels came and ministered to him. His mission became clear, and he returned to Galilee.

Meanwhile John the Baptist was speaking out against every kind of evil. He even condemned King Herod Antipas and his wife for their immoral marriage, which made the monarch and his wife furious. The king sent his soldiers to arrest John and throw him into prison, leaving the great number of John's followers without a leader. At that moment Jesus stepped forward and began preaching to the crowds; his message was even more dramatic than John's. He cried out: "The kingdom of heaven is drawing close. Repent and you can experience the fellowship of heaven now" (Mt 4:17, author's translation).

The Meaning of Heaven

Neither my childhood religious education nor my seminary training taught me much about heaven. Until I had spent many years in ministry, I did not fully realize that the kingdom of heaven or eternal life can touch us *now*. When death robbed me of my mother when I was twenty-one, life collapsed around me. In this period of confusion and darkness I decided I would go to the seminary to see if Christianity could show me any real meaning in this life. I left the theological school with the grand conviction that there were as many good reasons for believing in God as for not believing. And off I went into parish ministry, with the questionable goal of becoming the most successful minister that ever came to each church I served. Not surprisingly, after eight years I found myself in the dark abyss again. This time I could not crawl out; I had to get some help. Grace led me to a friend, who brought me to a Jew who had survived the Holocaust in Nazi Germany; this man knew that God and heaven were real. He also believed that the New Testament was a true account of Jesus' ministry and that the Holy One still could save us human beings. The man taught me how we can open ourselves to the spiritual world that surrounds us and penetrates our physical world.

As I read the gospels again, I saw that within this spiritual world the supreme reality is love. The divine Lover asks only that we open ourselves to that love and share it with others, expecting nothing in return. I began to really hear what Jesus was saying in Galilee, and I understood that this was the ultimate truth about human life, now and eternally.

I began to understand that the Bible and particularly the words of Jesus and other New Testament writers were describing this spiritual realm, the divine Love that has created us, and our universe. This spiritual world became physically present to us in Jesus of Nazareth. His central message was about the closeness of this realm. By his teaching and healing Jesus showed the nature of the kingdom of heaven. Then Jesus was betrayed and crucified, and he died. By rising again he showed that evil and death have no ultimate power over us. Jesus' life, death, and resurrection revealed that the realm of spirit was in the beginning, is *now*, and ever shall be, world without end. Reflecting on this, I began to see why so many nominal Christians are afraid to talk about death: they have not been touched by the kingdom of heaven *now*. So I began to search for all I could find out about heaven. I discovered a great deal about the eternal spiritual realm/fellowship/kingdom/reign.

Everywhere I turned I found agreement that the message and practice of Jesus were unique. None of the Hebrew prophets spoke with the same incredible good news that Jesus proclaimed. No other major religion gives the idea of the reign of Abba. In his remarkable book, *Jesus of Nazareth*, Günther Bornkamm points out that Jesus uses this word in his personal encounter with God. And since there was no Greek word with the same meaning, Paul and the early Greek Church continued to use this Jewish word (Rom 8:20, Gal 4:6).

The word *abba* was used in close-knit Jewish families, and it had the meaning that "daddy," "mommy," or "papa" have in English. This word expresses the way a small child would call out to a loving parent in joy or fear. The way that Jesus spoke this word in the Garden of Gethsemane as he faced crucifixion reinforces all that he taught about the tender, loving nature of God. The simple word *abba* speaks volumes about the nature of God and heaven. We can turn to the loving Creator as a small child turns to a genuinely loving parent — with confidence and trust. Jesus describes heaven (both now and eternally) as a home where both prodigal and elder brother are truly welcomed if they will simply come home. This heavenly

11

home is infinitely larger than our physical universe and kinder than any human home. It is the foundation upon which our world rests.

One reason we seldom hear the good news about the loving and powerful reality of heaven is that this reality is called by many different names in the New Testament. The words *heaven* and *heavenly* are used 232 times. The words *eternal* or *everlasting* life occur in 43 places. And then the ordinary words *life* and *to live* are used 74 times to describe heaven-life. (Heaven-life is real *living*.) *Resurrection* and *rising from the dead* describe entering heavenly life now or eternally, and are found 149 times. Finally, Jesus or his followers speak about the kingdom of heaven or God or just refer to *the* kingdom 136 times. All these words refer to the same eternal reality.

The New Testament is essentially a book about heaven, and it reveals what fellowship with the Holy One can be. Jesus summarizes these many references to heaven in nine verses in the beginning of the Sermon on the Mount. (Gandhi remarked many times that the teachings of Jesus were divine, no matter what else one might believe about Jesus.)

Jesus did not talk about a mystical flight of the alone to the alone. Although, as we shall see, finding the kingdom may involve such experiences, Jesus saw our final state as essentially a *fellowship*, not an aloneness. He stressed our social nature, the fact that we cannot be fully human unless we relate to each other. In the Lord's Prayer, Jesus used the word *our* over and over. He told *us* to pray to *our* Abba, to ask for *our* daily bread, and to be forgiven *our* sins. It is *we* who are to forgive those who sin against *us*, who ask that *we* may be spared the time of trial and that *we* may be delivered from evil. Jesus was emphasizing that human beings need each other as well as God if we are to be completely human and come to our full potential as sons and daughters of God.

The early Church used the image of the holy city, the new Jerusalem, to express the same meaning that Jesus referred to as the kingdom of heaven. Heaven, the Church stressed, requires that we love other human beings as well as God. As difficult as it sometimes is for me and my introverted nature to realize this, heaven requires sharing both ways. Our love for other humans is what opens us to deeper, more profound love for God. And as our love for God grows and deepens, we become more like God and more able to love all the shapes and sizes, kinds and colors and types of human beings who will one day live with us in the city of God. As C. S. Lewis stresses in his imaginative trip to heaven in *The Great Divorce*, heaven is a reality to which we must adapt and adjust, and one adjustment we must all make is to grow in loving and forgiving one another.

So love is the essential foundation of God and heaven. As we grow in love, the doors of the kingdom swing open to us. And to make that love concrete we need one another. Heaven is the state of being in which we develop and grow in relationship with other human beings around us. We can also relate to the communion of saints, those who have stepped beyond our mortal life. And we can have fellowship with the angelic beings, and with the loving Trinity as well. Love opens incredible experiences of heaven to us.

Opening Ourselves to Heaven

When his disciples asked Jesus how to pray, he answered with the Lord's Prayer. He told them to speak directly to their Abba in heaven. They were to ask Abba to shower holiness upon the whole world. They were to ask that the kingdom of heaven come upon earth so that earth becomes a heavenly place where all the needs of all of us may be met. The disciples were to forgive one another as they were forgiven by God. (Christianity is the only major religion that offers free forgiveness to all who recognize their need and ask for it.) They were to ask to be spared times of trial and to be delivered from the destructive powers of evil — the dark abyss of fear and hate and violence in which so many people live. They were to conclude with praise —for the kingdom, the power, and the glory of heaven belong to Abba.

Some disciples were asking about when heaven might come, and Jesus replied: "The kingdom is within you and among you." The actual word that Luke used means both *within* and *among*. It is not either/or but both/and (Lk 17:20-21).

We cannot separate these meanings. If the love of heaven is within us, we will inevitably want to share it with others and it will be among us. Many people have tried to make heaven exist on earth. But if they do not have the love and forgiveness and gentle humanness of heaven within them, they will come to utter frustration or disaster. Only those with the kingdom within them can enable the spirit of love to grow around them. When we do not share the living water of the kingdom with those around us, our well goes dry.

How can we open ourselves to this eternal realm? First of all, we need to stop our busyness and total immersion in the physical world — our obsession with lawns and checkbooks, with success and power. We need to stop and reflect, to be silent and listen. The silence reveals a presence; sometimes that presence will come in a dream or a crisis, but the presence embraces us as Abba did his prodigal son. And yet we know that as the Holy One is embracing the whole universe, Abba is also embracing each of us. When we relate to love, we are required to love others — friends and enemies, families and strangers — as we are loved. If we are to have the kingdom of heaven *within* us, we need to participate in the fellowship of heaven *among* us and serve and love one another. We need to ask in prayer this question: "Whom do I most need to serve?"

Jesus gave us the eucharist in order that we might have a taste of the fellowship of heaven now. Jesus gives himself to all of us in the sacrament, and we share the peace with each other. It is true that there are times when we experience the love of the risen Christ in the silence alone. But we do not complete that experience until we share it with others as unworthy of our love as we are of Christ's love. As we come together to worship at eucharist looking for those we can serve, then we find true peace.

Mother Teresa of Calcutta has summarized "kingdom living" in these words:

The fruit of silence is prayer,
The fruit of prayer is faith,
The fruit of faith is love,

The fruit of love is service,
The fruit of service is peace.

This is the pathway to the fellowship of heaven.

Jesus' Picture of Heaven

There is a delightful old French story about Acousin and Nicolette, who are very much in love. When the hero is chided by a priest about his affection for Nicolette and told that he might go to hell unless he takes care, Acousin replies, "Oh! I don't want to go to heaven and be stuck with the old men and beggars and cripples, the pious old maids. Let me go to hell where I'll find knights and warriors and people who are bold and adventurous. I want to go to the place where the ladies are beautiful and fun-loving, and where I won't be bored!" Caught up as we are by worldly values and worldly things, most of us share some of the same feelings. We even wonder what the point of heaven is if it is going to be like an old folks' home, with nothing to do and no place to go.

We need to admit to ourselves that such feelings and ideas, though common, are a product of immaturity. But there is another reason why most of us have them: We have not listened to the picture that Jesus gave us of God's kingdom. Jesus spoke about heaven so many times that we can get lost among all the images the New Testament provides. But an overall view reveals that the images fit together into a magnificent picture. A good, integrated picture of heaven is found in the beatitudes, as recorded in Matthew 5:3-12 and Luke 6:20-26. For our purposes, the longer and more developed version in Matthew offers a blueprint that shows how all the references to heaven fit together. Whether this passage is directly from the mouth of Jesus or a summary by those who knew him well makes little difference. Either way, Matthew's passage summarizes Jesus' teachings about the kingdom, about the qualities that make for blessedness or true happiness, and about the results that can be expected in heaven. The blessed or fortunate, Jesus says, are those who have been touched by heaven's love. They have opened themselves to the final and permanent reality found in the fellowship of heaven. (This passage from Matthew is so easily memorized that I believe these words came from Jesus' mouth and were part of the oral tradition shared by Paul in 1 Corinthians 13.)

Jesus' description of the nature of the fellowship of heaven, and of those human qualities that open us to it now and always, is very simple and comprehensive:

How blest are those who know they are poor in spirit;
    the kingdom of heaven is theirs.
How blest are the sorrowful;
    they shall find consolation.
How blest are those of a gentle spirit;
    they shall have the earth for their possession.
How blest are those who hunger and thirst
to see right prevail;
    they shall be satisfied.
How blest are those who show mercy;
    mercy shall be shown to them.
How blest are those whose hearts are pure;
    they shall see God.
How blest are the peacemakers;
    they shall be called the children of God.
How blest are those who have suffered persecu-

tion for the cause of right;
the kingdom of heaven is theirs.

(Mt 5:3-10, NEB altered)

I was meditating on this passage while preparing for All Saints Day, when it suddenly came to me that the result or reward is the same in the first statement and the last one: "the kingdom of heaven is theirs." These two identical promises enclose the other six like parentheses. It occurred to me that the six intervening statements are descriptions of God's kingdom, the fellowship of heaven. So in the whole passage, Jesus is telling us what heaven is really like. He is describing the kingdom of God — the kingdom of Abba. The loving, caring, father-mother God has provided an incredible eternal heaven for us, asking only that we accept and seek it. We can experience something of it now, and in eternity we will see it all clearly. Now we see through a glass darkly, but then we will see face to face.

Certainly the results that Jesus suggested don't happen very often on earth, except when the kingdom is fully within and among us. Those who mourn and are sorrowful are not often comforted and consoled in this life; usually they go right on finding life a painful struggle. The gentle in spirit, those who have been called the meek or the poor in spirit, do not noticeably inherit the earth in this world. The merciful often lose their shirts and come out on the short end of business deals. In view of the world hunger problem, it is quite clear that the hungry and thirsty are not always filled physically. And those who hunger for spiritual satisfaction, like Martin Luther King, often end up with a bullet in the head, or are abused in some degrading way. Jesus was quite naive if he believed that these first four rewards were frequent earthly ones — so naive that we should be wary of taking him seriously. The last two promises, however, do not really make sense except in the context of eternal life. It would certainly be wonderful to see God and be called sons or daughters in this world, but true fulfillment of this promise makes sense only in an eternal heaven.

In fact, the whole set of beatitudes makes real sense only if Jesus was describing the nature of heaven within us, among us, and beyond us. He did this by describing the actual qualities of a life which leads to heaven. Then he described the results which are found among those people who are able to live in contact with Abba, the risen Jesus, and the Holy Spirit.

We must live our present lives here and now, on this planet. And not even occasional direct encounters with the Holy One can make it possible for us on our own to fully live out the qualities of life that are called blessed in the beatitudes. We do better when we find a fellowship in which these attitudes are valued by those around us and we are given encouragement. Even then, however, our success in this life is only partial. Jesus was describing a way of life that is difficult to achieve in the here and now. But a striving for this kind of living ushers us into the kingdom. Thus, in the beatitudes Jesus gave us a picture of God's kingdom in a more complete way than anywhere else in his recorded teaching. Already now we can taste the reality of heaven, but ultimately we shall live fully within it.

Nearly all of Jesus' other statements about the kingdom can be related to the six qualities of the life named in the beatitudes. These six beatitudes summarize the hundreds of references to heavenly life that are scattered throughout the New Testament, and they give a direct description of what heaven is like. I know of no one better qualified to tell us about heaven than Jesus of Nazareth. His understanding carries weight even for people who do not accept the Christian belief that Jesus had a unique relationship with God and the kingdom of heaven. Men and women of spiritual discernment in nearly every religion and culture pay attention to Jesus' insights about spiritual reality as well as his map of the way that leads us into the heavenly domain.

We Shall Find Consolation

How blest are the sorrowful; they shall find consolation.

One of the biggest difficulties with our modern world is its ethic of success. We believe that the key to a happy and successful life is to keep up appearances and just whistle troubles away. This pathway, however, does not work very well, as we find out by listening to people in depth. Behind the pretended light-hearted facade of most people we find lives touched by agony and fear, by sorrow and pain. As Ian MacClaren once said, "Be kind, for everyone is bearing a heavy burden." In fifty years of counseling, I have never yet known anyone who did *not* bear some heavy burden of body or soul or mind. Few of us realize this truth because so few of us listen in depth to our neighbors. Few of us know ourselves and so we even ridicule those bearing burdens. Real discipline and courage are required if we are to listen and accept everything —good, bad, and indifferent — in us and among us. On the deepest level we are cut off from each other. And because of this, people in pain fear that they are somehow different from others, and this burden is added to the rest of their burdens.

Behind the cheerful masks of college students, one finds loneliness and fear and pain. In some ways the campus of a large university is one of the loneliest places in the world. My friend Kenneth Johnson, the builder of the enormous University of Massachusetts, confirmed what I experienced at Notre Dame.

Sickness, of course, plagues many, many lives, particularly as old age begins to drag our bodies down. But physical suffering is not the most devastating human affliction. Very few suicides are caused by physical suffering alone. It is rather mental, psychological, or spiritual anguish which makes people feel that they cannot go on any longer and drives them to suicide as a way out.

Sometimes we are so absorbed by the pain of losing a loved one that life seems empty and meaningless, filled only with an agony of loneliness. Boredom, too, can become an intolerable burden, leaving us to face the prospect of hours dragging interminably on toward aging and helplessness. In other cases, people are torn by the frustration of not being able to be what they wish to be, caught between desires that seem to be diametrically opposed to each other. Look deeply into almost any life and you will find there some tragedy which would make the plot of a real drama. One reason why tragedy played out upon a stage helps to relieve our burdens for a while is that it turns the spotlight away from us and shows that similar problems exist elsewhere. We feel that someone has listened to us and heard our pain.

The New Testament shows that Jesus often healed people at the same time that he told them about the kingdom of God. The two seemed to go hand in hand, as in Matthew 4:23 and 9:35. These healings of mental and physical illness were clearly seen as one evidence of the nearness of the kingdom and of the fact that it was breaking into people's lives. Gregory of Nyssa stated that the kingdom actually broke into the world in the resurrection of Jesus, and that the healing ministry of the Church was the first-fruits of that event.

In the beatitude about those who sorrow, Jesus suggested that in heaven we are healed of sorrow, comforted, and consoled. According to the beatitudes, in the kingdom we will find these burdens of pain and fear washed away, and new life will be given to us. This new life will be free from the downdrag of physical and psychological impediments. Something quite similar is described by people who come back from near-death experiences. Like Arthur Ford, who did not want to go back to "that beaten, diseased hulk" he had left behind in a hospital, people who have near-death experiences frequently resist returning to their bodies. Often, dying patients experience freedom from pain and almost joyous moods just before death. In his fine book, *The Light Beyond*, Raymond Moody describes experiences very close to the promise of consolation given in the beatitudes. We can expect even psychological pain to be cleansed from us. In near death experiences people often have the feeling of being totally remade and renewed. The dreams of dying people often portray a journey into bliss and joy beyond human imagination, a real resurrection to full life.

The Greek word "to console" is *parakalé*. It is the word from which "paraclete" or "comforter" is taken. In New Testament usage, *parakalé* means to encourage and strengthen by consolation, or to comfort. The Latin equivalent is *advoco*, from which we get our word advocate. The comforter or advocate is the one who takes our part and stands up for those who ask for help. Although comfort and consolation are often seen as only release from pain, Jesus was speaking of more than a pain-killer or a spiritual anesthetic. The person who is comforted is not just soothed and relieved of misery, but he or she is strengthened and resurrected, reconstituted and re-established. Comfort and help which don't get at the root of our difficulties would be cheap indeed.

Our English word "comfort" carries something of this meaning. It comes from the Latin phrase *cum fortis*, meaning "with strength," and the later word *conforto*, "to strengthen." The paraclete, the comforter, is the one who not only takes away our pain, but also helps us through to rebirth, renewal, and transformation. The "comfortable words" used in the Anglican Communion service following the people's confession of sin show this understanding. These are strengthening and renewing words spoken by Jesus and taken from the letters by Paul and John. Real comfort can help us to grow and find our place in the substantial life of the kingdom of heaven. This is what comfort is about. It is the help God gives us now in our present problems, and then fully as we set out on our new adventures toward his kingdom, ready to find the companionship of Abba and of those who have already entered this dimension of life, those on the other side of the communion of saints.

Truly believing this promise of consolation and comfort is very difficult for most of us. Even when we hear that some people have actually experienced this promise, we are not sure. We fear that the idea of life that is healed and renewed, of life without pain and frustration, may have developed just from our wish for something better than what we have. But this is far from true. In fact, we humans have trouble even imagining such a prospect until we are given a taste of it. Then we begin to see life more from God's perspective, from an eternal stance. Only when we come to realize that our lives are ultimately in God's loving hands are we able to see that much of our misery and inner agony are caused by our limited horizons. Sickness and betrayal, violence and war are so evident in our world that they often keep us from seeing that the resurrection of Jesus defeated evil in the world. We need to continue to look for every ray of light and cling to it.

The promise of consolation is a guarantee that the forces which have caused havoc among human beings and disrupted spiritual reality will not always have power. "The years the locust have eaten will be restored." The parts of ourselves that have been lost or damaged by evil will be given back to us. The kingdom of heaven is the place where evil loses its deadly power to destroy. Without the victory of

Jesus' resurrection, true believing in this promise of heaven would be difficult.

Heaven is also the reality in which our strength is renewed. We are comforted, in the sense of being built up and given a fresh start with new vigor and vision and drive. Many people, as they come to the end of their life, grow tired and lose their courage and their desire to go on. As they experience the kingdom of heaven, they find life renewed, charged with new energy and desire.

Heaven is the place of rebirth. It provides the right conditions for creative new life to take place. As the Revelation of John states, those who reach heaven through difficulties and sorrow will never again feel hunger or thirst or the sun's scorching heat. The Lamb who is at the heart of the eternal, the new Jerusalem, will be their shepherd and will guide them to the water of life, and God "will wipe every tear from their eyes. Death will be no more" (Rv 21:4). We can expect to enter this new reality filled with a vigor that will never wear out and ready for transformation. We need to do all we can here and now to eliminate those dark powers that mar human life. But we also need to have the confidence of the early Christian martyrs, who faced death in the arenas singing joyful songs and hymns. They knew they were entering the kingdom.

Possessors of the Earth

How blest are those of a gentle spirit; they shall have the earth for their possession.

How can the gentle spirits gain possession of the earth? What sense does this make? Even if it is possible for them to inherit the earth, what does this have to do with heaven?

Both God and heaven have a real interest in earth. Everywhere he went, Jesus proclaimed that the kingdom of heaven was reaching out to earth, trying to alter the state of things here. The idea of the incarnation — which is so basic to the Christian point of view — is that the Holy One seeks to have influence upon this earth. When men and women could not hear Divine teaching through the prophets, the Holy One came to earth as a baby in a manger so Jesus might share our humanity and show us by his life and teaching what heaven is like.

The Holy One created the universe so that human beings could evolve on earth and relate with love to the Creator and to one another. Some recent scientists have written that our universe was created to produce life, and that the flower of life is love. God went to a lot of trouble to bring heaven to earth. The humble, or the gentle in spirit, are those who are given the particular task of bringing this about. Perhaps this is why it happens so slowly. If we are to belong to the kingdom, we need to be brought to it gently. But gentleness of spirit is not to be confused with weakness or fear; true gentleness has the strength to know that love endures forever.

The Greek word translated as "possessors" or "inheritors" applied to property rights and control over an estate. "Heirs" are those who will come into an estate, who will eventually control that estate, use it and enjoy it. They do not have it now, but the time will come when it will be theirs and they will make it their own. In this sense the earth can be considered the inheritance of those in heaven. In God's good time they will possess earth as their own; they will be given the essence of the things of earth to use and enjoy. In the meantime they will help the owner of the estate by cultivating it, protecting it, and encouraging humankind to grow and become what they are capable of becoming.

The gentle-spirited heirs are those kindly spirits who help Abba provide the love this earth so desperately needs to have. It makes little difference whether we call them guardian angels or friends in the communion of saints. These are heavenly beings who watch over people and care for those who die. They are *carers*, whose task is to help us achieve the good for which we seek. George Eliot concluded her novel *Middlemarch* with these words: "That all is not so ill with you and me as it might have been is largely due to those who lived faithfully a hidden life and rest in unvisited tombs." Such beneficent influence comes not only from the actions of good individuals on earth but also from those who have entered eternity.

The deceased, particularly the gentle-spirited deceased, are the very ones who are given permission to exert a gentle and hardly perceptible influence upon those on earth who are open to such influence. Raymond Moody and Karlis Osis in their research and Billy Graham in his book on angels have described the experience of being met at the point of death by a deceased friend or loved one. The other person is there to help us make the transition, and apparently has been keeping watch over us all the time. I have personally felt this guidance after the death of my mother and then after the death of my son.

The truth expressed in this beatitude is also found in the Apostles' Creed in the words about the "communion of saints." In repeating our belief in this fellowship, we are affirming that even death cannot separate us from the loving deceased who follow Christ's way of love. In fact, after death some individuals may be closer to us than the next-door neighbors who are strangers to the way of Christ. Saint Ambrose spoke of the continued communication he had with his deceased brother Satyrus. And today, too, many people have quite clear visions of significant deceased friends and family. The deceased who are kindly spirits and have inherited the earth influence us in many ways, even though we hardly know it. Those in the heaven beyond the earth are not so separated from us as we sometimes think. By becoming more conscious of the spiritual realm, we can often become more aware of the presence and the influence the deceased in heaven have upon us. The Psalmist sang that we are only slightly lower than heavenly beings; we can already be in close contact with those who are in heaven.

True Satisfaction

How blest are those who hunger and thirst to see right prevail; they shall be satisfied.

It is perfectly obvious that those who hunger and thirst to see right prevail are not always satisfied on earth. But in heaven they are filled and satisfied. They know that earth will finally come to holiness and wholeness. For instance, Jesus spoke in his time about the equality of every individual, but it took nearly nineteen hundred years before *Christian* nations got the vision that slavery was a deep and abiding evil. It often takes a long time to bring the love of Christ to actuality on earth.

Real satisfaction almost always comes gradually. The word in Greek for "being filled" came from the word for hay and was used to describe cattle being filled and satisfied. This too is a gradual process. A cow does not get satisfied all at once; it goes on munching a bit at a time. The kind of satisfaction this beatitude describes is a gradual and growing state. It is the result of slowly munching away on the eternal hay of love. Too much too fast could well choke us.

In Luke's version of the beatitudes, Jesus says that the actual physical hunger and thirst of the unfortunate will be filled. They will no longer suffer deprivation and poverty. The search for righteousness, of course, starts with attempts to satisfy the physical needs of human beings. Martin Luther King was able to bring hope to the black people, because he realized that Christian righteousness involves the way people are treated in buses and restaurants and job placement. Mother Teresa has demonstrated in our day that Christians must attend to people's physical needs. In the Lord's Prayer, Jesus told us to pray for *our* daily bread, and we are far from our goal when a third of the world's children go to bed hungry each night.

There are other needs, however, besides physical ones. Some of the most miserable people I have known have been individuals of wealth who lacked for nothing physically. They were free from the wanting and needing that keep most of us occupied, and so they were faced by the emptiness of their lives and the despair that comes unless something is found to fill the void in each of us. The psychological emptiness of human beings and their other psychological needs are even harder to fill than physical needs.

People need to be cared for and loved if they are to be filled psychologically. And that means finding not only the God who loves us but also an earthly heaven, with our Lord at the center of it, where there is loving fellowship with other individuals like ourselves. Indeed, one of the reasons for the Church is to provide fellowship for lonely and hurting human beings; the Church is not a museum for saints but a hospital for sinners. When the Church accomplishes this, it makes real and present that heaven which we seek for on earth. It is notable that the first free hospitals in human history were created by the persecuted early Christians.

Like John Stuart Mill, many of us cannot intellectually conceive of a world that would satisfy us. Our rational thinking fails when we try to picture how our deepest and most central needs can be satisfied. We can, however, rely on poetic visions to describe heaven. As Augustine put it in the *Confessions*, God made us for God's own self, and we cannot know rest or satisfaction until we find it in God. While our minds possess images only of things we have known, we can allow these images to be transfigured and seen in the light of this new, heavenly level of reality. In *The Great Divorce*, C. S. Lewis presents a superb picture of heaven —although my personal intuition is that it will be easier for us to adjust to this reality than Lewis suggests.

The images that Jesus used were often commonplace, and yet they showed that the kingdom of heaven is a treasure that exceeds our wildest imagination. He described the kingdom as a treasure hidden in a field (Mt 13:44). He said it is like a pearl that is worth everything one owns (Mt 13:45). He compared it to a feast. The Galilean peasants cherished wedding feasts —like the one at Cana where Jesus performed his first miracle (Jn 2:1-12) — but Jesus stretched people's imagination to taste a *king's* wedding feast, or a great man's feast with all the unfortunate people in the countryside seated with him (Mt 22:1-14; Lk 14:15-24). Like a mustard seed or yeast (Mt 13:31-33; Mk 4:30-33; Lk 13:18-21), the kingdom of heaven provides more than seems possible. It fills and satisfies us far more than we could expect. The kingdom meets needs we don't even know we have.

Poets of almost every period, from the unknown creators of heroic epics to Blake and Kipling, have tried to give some picture of this spiritual reality. They have seemed to sense that without such a vision of heaven life goes flat and meaningless for many people. Virgil gave his vision of eternal things in *The Aeneid*, and Dante uses Virgil in *The Divine Comedy* as his guide through hell and purgatory. But it is Beatrice who leads Dante, at the end of his great epic, on to his final vision of heaven, which his own words cannot describe and where phantasy loses its power. In a flash Dante knows where his desire has come from, and he finds his will and his desire harmoniously turned by love, the love that moves the sun and the other stars. In this deepest vision of heaven, Dante tastes true and complete satisfaction. Another magnificent vision of heaven touching earth is the last scene of Goethe's *Faust*, where the Virgin Mother sends a host of angels to rescue Faust from the hands of Mephistopheles. Here, too, love is the ultimate reality.

In heaven we will no longer be frustrated and incomplete because of our inability to be what we wish to be. On earth, great misery is caused by our failure to become the kind of people we want to be. We build prisons of guilt for ourselves by condemning and castigating ourselves for failing to hit the mark that we have set for ourselves. In heaven we will at last be able to achieve our goals and become what we desire to be spiritually, psychologically, and morally. Neither defects of personality and mind nor weariness of body will get in the way.

Not only will the heavenly counterpart of physical need be filled, but our intellectual, moral, creative, and artistic desires will be satisfied as well. In heaven we will see clearly into the heart and center of things. To use Kiplings image, we will sit at a ten-league canvas and paint with brushes of comets' hair and be able to convey the visions of our hearts adequately. We will be able to love and forgive, to understand and help others as we have wanted to do on earth and yet haven't ever quite succeeded. We will be able to put off our pride and resentments, our hate and dislikes. Perhaps we will even be able to play the kind of chess game we have never yet managed, and share in some other divine, heavenly playfulness.

The best pictures we have of heaven suggest that we will be slowly transformed until we become the kind of people we have always wanted to be. Then we will find visions of new potentials and gradually move toward new goals. We will be filled, satisfied, utterly and eternally, and each filling will be more complete than the last. And those who have worked for the needy with love will be received triumphantly in heaven, as Vachel Lindsay suggests in his poem *General William Booth Enters Heaven*; he wrote this ecstatic vision to honor the founder of the Salvation Army.

Mercy and Love

How blest are those who show mercy; mercy shall be shown to them.

As I noted before, Christianity is the only major world religion that promises free forgiveness and mercy to anyone who genuinely asks for it. But most of us, sadly, have had just enough taste of the mercy which Christianity promises to be immunized against accepting and understanding it. I get so discouraged with Christian ministers who preach judgment, and more judgment, when the essential message of Christianity is loving mercy and forgiveness.

Most people are already judging themselves far too much, and they cannot imagine being forgiven. Preaching judgment or acting it out only walls people off from us and shuts them up with their problems. Judging is very close to the essential idea of *karma*, which says that individuals must pay for every sin and error they have committed. Reflecting on my own life, I hope and pray that this is not so. Over the years I have learned a great deal about how retribution and self-hatred drive us further and further from salvation. I am very sure that judgment and punishment seldom, very seldom, redeem anyone.

God is not only just; the Holy One is merciful. Heaven is not a place of retribution, but a place of forgiveness, mercy, healing, and love. Here, again, this idea is not just wish fulfillment, something we have made up out of whole cloth. On the contrary, it is beyond the fondest hopes of most human beings on this earth until they are introduced to it. And it takes work to open us up to any glimmering that such love and mercy might be waiting to embrace us.

We humans do not even begin to look for absolute forgiveness from God unless we have been treated with at least some forgiveness by the people around us. Only as we are loved and forgiven in our ordinary lives do we begin to understand dimly that this is what God and heaven are like. It is practically impossible to believe in the ultimate reality of the forgiveness of sins unless we have known it here and now. There is probably no belief in the Apostles' Creed which is harder for us humans to accept than the eternal forgiveness of sins.

In ordinary life we forget that the idea of mercy has been expressed in the Christian tradition from the beginning. One example is the Jesus' prayer used in Christian devotion. For centuries this prayer, in one form or another, has been a central practice of Orthodox devotion. To pray this prayer, we simply say over and over to ourselves these words: "Lord Jesus Christ, Son of God, have mercy on me, a sinner." By constant, almost incessant repetition, we make the reality of mercy a foundation of our lives. Both the *Philokalia*, a standard work of Eastern monasticism, and the popular devotional classic *The Way of a Pilgrim* show clearly how creative this practice has been in the Orthodox tradition. I find the prayer in its simplest form — "Jesus, mercy" — of incredible help in dark and dangerous times. The *Kyrie eleison* —Lord, have mercy; Christ, have mercy; Lord, have mercy — is said or sung in most Christian liturgies, usually following our confessions of failures. These practices suggest how central the idea of mercy is in any real Christianity.

Hell, as someone has said, can be described as a state of eternal obsession with guilt so that we are unable to accept forgiveness. The flames of hell are then the rejected flames of God's love, as Catherine of Genoa held. By this definition we all have at least one foot in hell. I have known no one who did not at some time need God's mercy and love. The few who *thought* they didn't need any mercy have been the very ones who needed it most. Even the murderous Macbeth and his wife might have escaped their hell if they had been able to admit their need for forgiveness, but then Shakespeare would not have written his great tragedy. Life becomes tragic when we will not forgive or accept forgiveness. The unique idea of Christianity is that humans do not need to suffer from guilt and self-condemnation; we can be forgiven any and every wrong-doing if we are truly sorry and truly try to remedy the situation. We then sincerely seek mercy and forgiveness — and also forgive all those who have harmed us. Heaven is the state of being — the *place*, in metaphorical language — in which we can be washed free of guilt and given a fresh start by divine mercy. In Shakespeare's last three plays, potential tragedy is averted when the characters forgive each other.

The Greeks had two sets of words relating to mercy. Those words associated with the noun *oiktos* were used generally to speak of emotional reactions, feelings of pity or sorrow, and such a word is found only a few times in the New Testament. The other noun for mercy or compassion was *éleos*, which indicated emotion that brought action and some kind of help for a tragic situation. The Greeks even worshiped Éleos as a divine being embodying the qualities of mercy. This is the word found in the beatitudes and in many other places in the New Testament. When these passages are considered together, the meaning is quite clear: The person to whom mercy is shown is rescued and restored. This beatitude could be translated: "Blest are the merciful, for they shall be restored." And the merciful are those who will be able to give this kind of mercy freely, without looking for anything in return.

In the story of the prodigal son, this is the meaning of the ring which the father places on the son's finger. Undoubtedly the ring has been set with an engraved stone, which gives the son authority over family property again. We have heard this story so often that we are no longer amazed by its wild extravagance, its incredible mercy. Often we do not even hear what Jesus was saying — that heaven is the place where prodigals are welcomed if only they will get up from their pigsties and come home. They are given not only authority but a joyous banquet and honor as well. Kenneth Bailey has called attention to the incredible mercy portrayed by this story in his remarkable little book, *The Cross and the Prodigal*. (It is important to remember that jealous elder brothers can be forgiven also. All they have to do is to accept the invitation, relax, and come to the party.)

There are very few people who ever receive such mercy in this life, even from their families (in many cases particularly not from their families). Forgiveness is another radical Christian promise that is beyond the wildest hopes or expectations of most of us. It is true that people need glimpses of human forgiveness in order to believe in the absolute forgiveness of God, but the reverse is also true: Unless we are taught that the Holy One and heaven are infinitely merciful, we usually make God in the image of the unforgiving humans we have known. We then imagine that we will meet a God of judgment and retribution when we pray or when we go beyond our mortal span.

How seldom do we realize that eucharist is the feast for both prodigals and elder brothers who have been willing to come home, but the eucharist is precisely such a feast. In our Holy Communion we ask for mercy, and we offer one another forgiveness in the passing of peace. This is a sign of our sharing in the mercy of God that we will receive from the divine table. Then we are given the mercy and love in the sacrament, and we are made whole.

In parable after parable, Jesus tried to make clear God's mercy and the nature of heaven. But people very seldom ask for and receive this kind of mercy and renewal unless they can imagine that God and heaven might be this wonderful. I often found it impossible to even reach my own children with the kind of mercy I wanted to give them unless they first could come to me expecting it. As I have described in *The Other Side of Silence*, and *Set Your Hearts on the Greatest Gift*, it takes a certain courage and humility to ask for and receive mercy. Mercy is given to those who know their need of the Divine Spirit described in the first beatitude; their deepest needs are filled and their deepest sorrows removed. In heaven their lives are fulfilled in much the same way as the lives of those who hunger and thirst after righteousness are fulfilled.

Those who have received mercy know what it is to be loved by God, and so they allow the divine Lover to penetrate the deepest recesses of their hearts and lives. John of the Cross described this experience in his *Stanzas of the Soul*. In these lines he tried to put into images his experience of finding Christ during a time of persecution. These images, I believe, give us his preview of the nature of heaven:

> Oh, night that guided me.
> Oh, night more lovely than the dawn,
> Oh, night that joined Beloved with lover,
> Lover transformed in the Beloved!
> Upon my flowery breast,
> Kept wholly for himself alone,
> There he stayed sleeping, and I caressed him,
> And the fanning of the cedars made a breeze.
> The breeze blew from the turret
> As I parted his locks;
> With his gentle hand he wounded my neck
> And caused all my senses to be suspended.
> I remained, lost in oblivion;
> My face I reclined on the Beloved.
> All ceased and I abandoned myself,
> Leaving my cares forgotten among the lilies.

Austin Farrer has also written of a similar encounter with Christ, describing his experience in these words:

God forgives me, for he takes my head between his hands and turns my face to his to make me smile at him. And though I struggle and hurt those hands — for they are human, though divine, human and scarred with nails — though I hurt them, they do not let go until he has smiled me into smiling; and that is the forgiveness of God.

This is the way divine Love treats us now and in eternity. This is what it is like to be loved fully and to be given mercy. Experiences like these can be found in our deepest meditations. They give us a foretaste of the life which stretches before us eternally. Such experiences help us realize that we can encounter the same reality and find just such love and mercy when we make our transition to the other side of the communion of saints.

Few of us have ever been fully listened to, let alone truly loved with mercy. Those who are actually given this kind of compassion by some other human being begin to know what it is to be reborn within this present life. Very likely we will experience such re-birth again and again as new levels within us keep opening up and are transformed by mercy. Mercy is ongoing and eternal.

The Vision of God

How blest are those whose hearts are pure;
they shall see God.

One by one the descriptions of heaven in the beatitudes touch our hearts like waves beating on the shore. Our hearts jump with joy at the promise that those who are pure in heart shall behold God. This is still another way of speaking of the fulfillment of our earthly striving, the satisfaction of our desires. There is nothing that a lover wishes more than to catch a glimpse of the beloved who has been away and returns. Our hearts are set on fire. We shall at last come face to face with the only Love that lights our entire inner being.

Love is given to us to draw us toward God. Those who have never been head over heels in love can seldom imagine the consummation which is given in meeting the divine Lover. Our human love is only a shadow of that love which draws all that exists to itself with infinite tenderness and gentle patience.

We humans celebrate our love in poems and stories. Few things stir us as deeply as a really good love story, but none of our human tales equal the divine love story. Most of the time we simply don't believe the incredible good news. Only the greatest poets and storytellers can give a sense of it without maudlin sentimentality. C. S. Lewis had this ability. In his Narnia novels, beginning with *The Lion, the Witch and the Wardrobe*, he uses the image of the divine lion, Aslan, who guides and protects four children through daring adventures beyond this world. Aslan is sacrificed to save the child who has betrayed the others. The children's grief is boundless, but when Aslan is raised again, the joy of the children at finding him alive points to the meaning of the beatitude we are discussing. All who single-mindedly drawn toward God can behold the holy now and eternally.

Mystics in every period have spoken of the beatific vision, of seeing or experiencing the divine. This is one pole of the divine encounter, the one expressed in this beatitude, with the opposite pole represented by the beatitude that follows. The essence of the beatific vision is an experience of joy in which every care is forgotten. This experience is often imageless, or sometimes we become aware of a brilliant light, so intense that it normally would hurt our eyes. Sometimes we meet the risen Christ, who takes away all fear and gives us a taste of heaven now. This is the moment of coming to the center, finding the reality that is there, the source of all things, and knowing that we are forgiven, accepted, desired, loved, fulfilled.

Those who have this experience can come to an awareness of the kingdom and realize that the reality they have encountered asks only one thing of them. They need to reach out and share with others the love and peace and strength which they have experienced, allowing the fabric of their being to radiate divine love. On earth this means they must go out to the highways and byways, into their families and churches, their offices and clubs, bearing this kind of love. In heaven it means taking their places as sons and daughters of God, brothers and sisters of Christ, ready to act as agents of the Holy Spirit.

The spirit of God moves in a pulsating rhythm. We need our moments of ecstasy and quiet adoration, and also times of action and reaching out. Unless we have both, we lack the balance and wholeness that indicate spiritual health. Those who emphasize only one aspect of the spiritual life, of heaven, and look down on the other aspect do not share the fullness of healthy kingdom living. The spirit and heaven are both static and moving. We need *both* moments of pure vision and rest and enjoyment *and* moments of bringing love to the hungry, the dying, the lonely, and those who love us. We can be quite sure that such a heaven will never be boring.

These glimpses of the utter joy of the kingdom — of heaven — and its power can come in many different ways: as a sense of being lifted out of ourselves by a loving power, as an experience of the risen Jesus, or as a sense of the angelic realm. These different kinds of experience are recorded throughout the Bible. Abraham, for example, was called by God; Moses met God in the burning bush; Paul was transformed on his trip to Damascus, where he was bent on vengeance. Paul, of course, became one of the most active apostles; he was also lifted to an indescribable third heaven (Acts 9; 2 Cor 12). Cornelius and Peter were given divine messages that led Peter to establish a mission to the Gentiles (Acts 10). When Stephen was being stoned, the heavens opened and he saw Jesus standing at the right hand of the Holy One (Acts 7:54-60).

These experiences still happen today. One careful survey revealed that thirty-nine percent of those questioned had experienced transforming religious encounters. However, when these people were questioned later, half of them revealed that they had never told anyone else about these experiences; they feared that they would be subject to ridicule in our materialistic society. Within the last year I wrote an introduction to G. Scott Sparrow's book, *I Am With You Always*, produced by a mass-market publisher; it describes hundreds of life-changing visions of the risen

Jesus in our times. Several years ago, at a conference of some two hundred people, I asked those present to write down their most significant religious experiences; I received fifty accounts of transforming encounters with the divine, some of which changed the people's lives. Physical and emotional healings occurred in many of these encounters. These visions of the divine can come totally unexpectedly. They can happen as we meditate or as we face our darkness and cry for help. They also occur to people who are close to death. The single-minded seekers (the pure of heart) probably receive such confirmations of the kingdom more often than any other group on the spiritual journey.

Few theologians or religious writers deal with these visions of the kingdom of heaven. However, one fine religious writer had a remarkable encounter during what could have been a fatal accident. Henri Nouwen relates what happened to him as he looked for the first time at what might be beyond this mortal, physical dimension of life.

> He was there, the Lord of my life, saying, "Come, don't be afraid. I love you." His presence was deeply human as well as deeply divine, very personal but so much greater than my imaginings. I knew without doubt that he was there for me, but also that he was embracing the universe. I knew he was the Jesus I prayed to and had spoken about, but also that now he did not ask for prayers or words. All was well.

The words that summarize it all are *life* and *love*. But these words were incarnate in a real presence. Death lost its power and shrank before the Life and Love that surrounded me in such an intimate way.

One emotion was very strong — that of home-coming. Jesus opened his home to me and seemed to say, "Here is where you belong." The words he spoke to his disciples became very real:

"There are many rooms in my Father's house. . . . I am going now to prepare a place for you" (Jn 14:2, JB). The risen Jesus, who now dwells with his Father, was welcoming me home after a long journey.

My homecoming had a real quality of return, a return to the womb of God. The God who had fashioned me in secret and molded me in the depths of the earth, the God who had knitted me together in my mother's womb, was calling me back and *wanted to receive me as someone who had become child enough to be loved as a child.*

(*Beyond the Mirror* [New York: Crossroad, 1990].)

The Children of God

How blest are the peacemakers; they shall be called the children of God.

The peacemakers, Jesus said, will be called the children of God (literally God's "sons," but, given

Jesus' view of women, this unquestionably includes God's daughters as well). There are moments when one needs to become a child and merely rest in the everlasting arms. One of the richest memories of life with my own children goes back many years to the night before one of my sons was to leave for college. I often retire early to meditate and rest; on that evening my son came into my room quietly and lay down beside me with his head on my chest. There were no words. After about half an hour he got up and went to his own room. The memory of those quiet moments together is priceless, and at the same time they remind me of other times when one of the children worked along with me at some task, with obvious delight. They knew that they could share with me and that they were loved.

These experiences tell something about our relationship with God now and about how it will be in heaven eternally. As children of God, we will know quiet rest in the Holy One, and we will also be able to be fully active as God's helpers. We will work along with the Holy One without becoming weary, sharing in the infinite divine projects of love. We will learn the meaning of the phrase in the ancient prayer for peace: "whose service is perfect freedom." In heaven we can expect, as sons and daughters of God, that our work will be like the pure play of children, full of joy, fun, and excitement. In this way we will grow and develop, learning and serving, and then come to rest again on the breast of the divine Lover, as John of the Cross describes so magnificently in his poem.

Jesus gives a graphic description of heaven and the life beyond physical existence in the parable about

Lazarus, the beggar, and then in his reply to the Sadducees who tried to trap him on the question of the resurrection of the dead.

In the parable, Jesus describes a rich man (who is not even named). He has all of the material comforts of a good life. He dines sumptuously every night. His guests clear their plates with pieces of bread and then throw the scraps to the dogs. At the rich man's door lies a poor beggar, Lazarus, who longs for the bits of bread that are thrown to the dogs, and no one even notices him. He is unclean because the dogs come to lick his sores. (It is important to realize that the rich man's fault is not that he is rich but that he blindly ignores the suffering person at his door [Lk 16 :19-31].)

Both men die. Lazarus is carried away by angels to lie on Abraham's bosom or chest; he has expected nothing and is so much a child that now he can be loved as a child by Abraham, the father of the chosen people, and by God. The rich man has a lavish burial, but his blindness to the beggar's misery and hunger keeps him from resting in the eternal kingdom. (Most of us in first-world countries are richer than the rich man in Jesus' time. We need to ask ourselves if we are indeed caring for the hungry and sick who lie at our door. We need to remember Jesus' words: "Just as you did to the least of my brothers and sisters, you have done to me" [Mt 25:40, author's translation].)

Jesus' notable reply to the Sadducees occurred when the Sadducees were trying to make Jesus' look ridiculous because he taught that we can get a vision of the kingdom of heaven now and that we continue to *live on* in an even better eternal life. To trip Jesus up, the Sadducees told a story of a woman whose husband was one of seven brothers. When the husband died leaving no children, the Mosaic law required that the second brother must marry her and raise up children for the deceased brother. However, the second husband also died without any children. In turn each brother married the woman and then died, and then the woman also died still childless. The Sadducees asked: "At the resurrection, whose wife will the woman be?"

Jesus replied: "Those who belong to this age marry and are given in marriage; but those who are considered worthy of a place in that age and in the resurrection from the dead neither marry nor are given in marriage. Indeed they cannot die anymore, because they are like the angels and are children of God, being children of the resurrection." Jesus then referred his opponents to their own law, to Moses' experience at the burning bush where the Holy One told Moses: "I am the God of Abraham, Isaac and Jacob." Jesus concluded that the Holy One of Israel is not the God of the dead, but of the living, and that all the patriarchs are still alive (Lk 20:27-39; Mt 23:23-33; Mk 12:18-27). Jesus answered with such depth and penetration that no one dared to ask him any further questions.

On another occasion the Pharisees were horrified when Jesus called himself the Son of God. Jesus told them that they did not understand our spiritual value, and then he quoted scripture again:

Is it not written in your own Law, "I said: You are gods"? Those are called gods to whom the word of God was delivered — and scripture cannot be set aside. (Jn 10:34-35)

Jesus was saying that the sons and daughters of God possess the same spiritual nature as the angels, agents of the divine whom God also created. This is the high density of heaven, which Jesus later emphasized to the disciples in a personal way. He told them:

You are my friends, if you do what I command you. I call you servants no longer; a servant does not know what his master is about. I have called you friends, because I have disclosed to you everything that I heard from my Father. (Jn 15:14-15)

Friends and adult children are in the same category; they share the confidence and life and work of the parent and friend. This is the relationship between God and God's people, now and in heaven.

One of the most delightful ways that Jesus pictured heaven was in terms of a feast and, even better, a royal wedding party: "From east and west people will come, from north and south, for the feast in the kingdom of God" (Lk 13:29-3:29, NEB). A feast is not only an occasion for filling oneself with food, but a time for exuberance, fellowship, fun, joy. Those who refuse to come to the party and celebrate, like the elder brother in the story of the prodigal, or those who make excuses for not coming, will have to change their attitudes and learn to enjoy others' good fortune before they can participate in the kingdom. Jesus evidently did not expect us to be working or just resting with God all of the time. Times for playing with God are a necessary addition, because eternal anything — working, resting, thinking, *or* playing —would soon become dull.

Our capacity to play may be more essential to our being human than our thinking capacity. Perhaps the Holy One created this amazing universe — this universe of whirling galaxies, of mysterious tiny sub-atomic particles that defy our understanding — just for the joy of a song. The playfulness of God strikes us when we look at the strange and colorful birds and fish and animals. Our universe is the result of loving divine creativity and play.

Andrew Greeley pictures the playfulness of God with a vision patterned after a grand Irish drinking party. Greeley quotes from an anthology of Irish literature these words from the tenth century:

> I should like to have a great pool of ale for the
> King of Kings; I should like the Heavenly Host
> to be drinking it for all eternity.

Children, sons and daughters, not only rest with their parents, they work and play with them; similarly, in heaven we can expect joy and fulfillment as well as work and play in furthering the kingdom.

Is Heaven Worthwhile?

Using the framework provided by the beatitudes, we can describe quite a bit of what heaven is like. It is that state of being in which we shall be comforted, made heirs to all of the earth's richest treasure, filled to the brim so that our deepest longings are satisfied. It is that eternal dwelling where we shall receive mercy, pardon, restoration, and rebirth. Then we shall behold the Holy One and work and play with the company of heaven, with those who allow Divine Love to touch them. This is heaven. Boethius once summed it all up in one sentence: *Heaven is the simultaneous fruition of life without bounds*.

Heaven is like a bud bursting into eternal bloom, and a blossom ripening into eternal fruit. And then the process of bud and bloom and fruition starts over, again and again. Heaven is like emerging from a dark tunnel into the full light of day. It is like the bright sky we find as our plane rises through the clouds and smog to find the light of sun shining on us.

Is heaven worthwhile? An old hymn sings: "Heaven is my home; I'm just a pilgrim here below." Is the holy city worth the pilgrimage, the harbor worth the voyage?

You can tell much about a family by the way they have furnished and decorated their house. You can tell much about a public place by the people who frequent it, and about a city or a country by the people who come from it. We can tell much about heaven by the people we know are there. Heaven is the place where we will find those kindly, fine, noble, courageous, self-effacing, humble, understanding, forgiving, striving spirits whom we have loved on earth. It is the place and state of being where they are happy and at home. Such a place certainly looks very worthwhile.

Now let us look at those who have become part of the communion of saints. The beatitudes describe the people to be found in heaven. These people will give us an insight into how we can prepare for the kingdom of heaven.

Preparing for Eternal Life

We do not share in the kingdom of heaven by attaining power or success in the secular world, by athletics, money, or popularity. The way to heaven is not based on the world's standards of "success"; the way of Jesus Christ is topsy-turvy by ordinary human standards. Even the people who are powerful and intelligent and strong, who are able to live ascetic or religiously correct lives entirely on their own, are not the first ones to be received into the divine fellowship. We do not get into heaven, Jesus told us, because we are wise and know enough to get there on our own, but because we are childlike and seeking and aware of our inadequacies. A place is reserved in heaven for the dispossessed and unfortunate, the gentle and the merciful. The words of the *Magnificat*, first spoken by Mary before Jesus' birth, put it very clearly. These words are one of the great hymns of the Christian fellowship:

His name is Holy;
> his mercy sure from generation to generation toward those who fear him.

The deeds his own right arm has done disclose his might: the arrogant of heart and mind he has put to rout,
> he has torn imperial powers from their thrones, but the humble have been lifted high.

The hungry he has satisfied with good things, the rich sent empty away.

(Lk 1:49-53, NEB).

These words present obvious problems. We live in a world that requires ego strength. Even the Holy One seems to expect us to use our own strength as far as we can to keep our earthly house in order. God even seems to boost our self-assurance at times: God anticipates the mistakes we will make in trying to grow spiritually and to act lovingly, and the Holy One gives us unlimited forgiveness so we can make fresh starts and try again and again. The trouble is that our ability to fend for ourselves, even in limited ways, tends to give us a sense of power that can cut us off from God and heaven.

We are on a tightrope, a narrow path. If we fail to use the human resources that are available to us and sidestep our responsibilities in this world, we may find ourselves turning away from heaven entirely. On the other hand, if we go ahead on our own with self-satisfied pride and are successful in avoiding most wrongdoing and living up to the highest standards, it is all too easy for us to think we are headed for heaven when all we are doing is staying on a safe, well-traveled path that leads nowhere.

How then can ordinary individuals like you and me prepare for that dimension of reality which we call heaven, where we may meet Abba and become instruments of divine love? The descriptions of those whom Jesus called blessed in the beatitudes point the way. I have shown that Jesus statements were quite clearly intended to describe more than just the kind of people who may be found in the realm of the communion of saints. They are also meant to show us the kinds of attitudes and actions that will give us a vision of that kingdom in the here and now. And these are also the attitudes and actions that will prepare us to share fully in that same kingdom eternally.

These eight qualities of life are not steps on a stairway which everyone must take one after another to reach this fortunate or blessed state. They are more like eight different doors, any one of which can swing open and let us enter the fellowship of the kingdom. Abba does not require us to be totally integrated and to have all the virtues in order to find a place in the heavenly kingdom. Holy love asks only that we take the right road for us and try to find at least one of these eight entryways. Each of these doors into life is related to all the others.

Each of us has a characteristic redeeming quality. It has been said that those of us who experience the world mainly through sensation, the sensing types, have the virtue of simplicity, while intuitive people possess wisdom, thinking types are notable for their justice, and feeling people are characterized by joy. Each of us, then, has a unique way of approaching the kingdom, and each of us must move toward the doorway that will swing open and welcome us. Let us look at the eight ways that Jesus described in the beatitudes and see what patterns of life they suggest. We need to develop our natural bent first and then later work at other ways to develop a balanced life. We have all eternity to grow and become fulfilled.

Beggars in the Spirit

Those who know their need for God, the poor in spirit, are literally "beggars." The Greek word used in the beatitudes is *potchós*, which came from a verb meaning to skulk, to cringe or cower in fright, to live by begging. Originally it applied only to the indigent who had to beg to live, those in actual economic want. This word had very negative connotations in the ancient Greek world. The poor and sick were those who were being punished by the gods. Until Christianity opened up a new attitude toward poverty, beggars were pictured as the refuse of society, wandering about in contemptible wretchedness. The first time this word was used in a positive way in Greek literature was in the New Testament. The story Jesus told about the beggar lying helpless at the rich man's door (Lk 16:19-31) is striking in that this beggar is not despicable but is, rather, headed for heaven. He is blessed. Used in this way, "beggar" had come to mean a person who is destitute or impoverished in any way — in wealth, influence, position, honor, self-esteem, or spiritual value. Beggars know their need or they would not be begging!

In Luke's beatitudes the word for beggar stands alone, while in Matthew it is followed by "in the spirit." Matthew is emphasizing that "beggar" does not refer only to people who are poor in an outer way (although it includes them), but to those who are inwardly poor, who seem to get nowhere spiritually no matter how hard they try, who are not self-satisfied. In most places Jesus made it very clear that in speaking of poverty, he was talking about an inner quality. While physical poverty often leads to poverty of spirit, this is not always true. Unless that inner quality is present, lack of the good things of this life can result in anger, violence, and projection. People can become just as proud of poverty as they often are of their talents or powers or possessions, thus robbing poverty of value. Wealthy individuals, furthermore, have been known to refuse help to the poor for the hypocritical reason that their poverty will bring blessings. We humans can distort Jesus' meaning with incredible ease.

So although it is inexcusable to romanticize poverty and hence to fail to aid the poor, it is true that among the very poor there is often a sense of detachment from life which opens them to another dimension of reality. The poor have so little to hang onto except life itself that they are not dominated by worldly attachments.

The same thing is true of people who come to know real *inner* poverty and are forced to realize that they cannot survive by their own strength and wisdom. These individuals have learned that they must have the help of a divine, spiritual power greater than themselves in order to survive at all. They have come to know the complexity of their inner worlds, the shadow and evil that dwell in the hearts of the best and most spiritual of us. They know the incredible conflicts within their own psyches and realize that they cannot bring themselves together to cope with such a life without saving help. My own experience has shown me that I do not often turn to the risen Christ because I am virtuous, but because I cannot manage my life without him. This is what is meant by being "poor" or a "beggar" in spirit. I come to the love and mercy of Jesus because I cannot survive without them and I can find them nowhere else.

Few of us who will read these words have ever known actual poverty, even those who live in religious communities. It is hard for us to imagine being completely dispossessed, like the peasants of Jesus' time and our time — at the mercy of both wealthy landlords and the petty officials of a foreign government. Most of us have no comprehension of what it meant to be a beggar in that day, to be utterly dependent on other people's charity. Beggars knew that they had to have help if they were to survive and that this help had to come from beyond themselves as a pure gift or grace. But individuals who become lost in inner anxiety and turmoil, hopelessness and depression do know something of the same poverty of spirit. They know that they lack the resources to make it on their own.

Jesus had a great deal to say about what would happen to people who are at the bottom of the heap in this world. Several times he made the point that the first will be last and the last first. This is the point of his story of the workers in the vineyard who come late in the day and are still paid a full day's wages (Mt 20:1-16). Jesus illustrated the same idea to the disciples by taking a small child in his arms, showing how those who want to be first must become like servants to those who have the least (Mk 9:33-37). He also told people not to take the places of honor at a wedding feast but to sit in the lowest seats, because those who humble themselves will be lifted up (Lk 14:8-11). And in his parable of the last days, when people will be separated like sheep from goats, Jesus identified those who ministered to the lowliest and the most downtrodden as those who were ministering to him (Mt 25:31-46).

When the Pharisees and scribes complained that he was friendly with sinners (Lk 15), Jesus told in parables how God seeks after the lost. He used the parables of the lost coin, the lost sheep, and particularly the lost son to show that those who know their lostness and despair are the very ones who can be found and restored. God seems to hanker after these lost ones because of their inner misery and need. This was apparently what Jesus recognized in such despised tax collectors as Zacchaeus, whom he sought out (Lk 19:2-10), and Matthew, whom he chose as a disciple (Mt 9:9). As tax collectors, they were both considered spiritually lost and treasonous, beggars in spirit.

This idea is found again and again in the gospels. The surest way to gain one's life or one's self-esteem is to lose it, while those who continue to put their own pride and self-conceit first will end up losers (Mt 10:39; 16:25; 18:4; 23:12; Mk 8:35; Lk 9:24; 14:11; 17:33; 18:14; Jn 12:25). People who know that they are inferior and despised and outcast, the prostitutes and tax collectors, will enter the kingdom before those whose only virtue is that they scrupulously obeyed the religious law (Mt 21:31).

John Sanford calls attention to the understanding of Gregory of Nyssa about the lost. Gregory wrote that some individuals have lost the divine image within, that image which the fashioner of each individual heart has stamped upon our inner being. When they recover that image, they are so glad to have the presence of the divine in their hearts again that the experience brings them to the glory of the kingdom of heaven.

What does all of this mean for us today? It means that our most valiant efforts to hold the right beliefs and to do the right thing will come to naught if we become self-satisfied, judging and arrogant. The moment we think we are worthy of God's favor, the door to spiritual development slams shut. Entry into the kingdom (or coming to wholeness and maturity, which is this world's nearest equivalent of the kingdom of heaven) is in part a pure gift. Those who can accept it as a gift, unearned and unmerited, will be able to receive it fully. All the saints confessed that they were the worst of sinners.

In *The Great Divorce*, C. S. Lewis tells a story which illustrates this fact superbly. A group from hell have been given an excursion into heaven, and among them is a man whose vices were minimal, and whose virtues were equally minimal. The first person he meets in heaven is a murderer he had known. The visitor is obviously upset and he complains bitterly, screaming that he has never broken the law or cheated anyone. He concludes his tirade with: "All I want is my rights."

The murderer replies that if it were a matter of rights, *he* would not be in heaven: "I am here only through the bloody mercy of Jesus Christ." He goes on to explain that God gives us far better than we deserve, and he urges the visitor to accept forgiveness and stay there with him. But the visitor answers: "Im not asking for anybodys bleeding charity." And he turns his back on heaven and mercy and returns to hell, unable to comprehend what God offers.

God is so much more than we can imagine, so holy and pure and whole. We cannot rise to that level by ourselves, but God is also more merciful than we can imagine. He longs to give us more than we can dream of asking for. He wants to give us the fullness of heaven, but the gift can be received only if we are willing to accept it. If we continuously look back at our familiar homeplace and refuse to give up our cherished possessions, which are represented by the rights and virtues and pride that seem so important to us in this world, then we often cannot recognize and move on to the better things as they are offered to us by the kingdom.

There was a time when many people felt that they could make themselves inwardly poor by excessive asceticism. Even John of the Cross wore a chain around his middle with spikes to dig into his flesh. Sleeping on nails and mortifying the flesh may make one feel poor in spirit, but these practices are more likely to express self-hate and self-punishment than inward poverty. They are often difficult to distinguish from symptoms of psychological illness.

However, very few serious Christians engage in this kind of asceticism. Many of the finest followers of Christ have recommended a *positive* "penance" — loving all other human beings as God has loved us. A nun working with Catherine of Siena wrote to her leader asking how she might show her gratitude to the Holy One, who had given her such mercy, joy, and peace. Catherine wrote back, telling her that doing more penance and developing thicker callouses on her knees from prayer would not express her gratitude. Building the finest church in the world would not clearly express her gratitude either, as she could not add anything to the glory of the divine creation. However, she could show her gratitude to God by loving those as unworthy of her love as she was of

God's love. Positive asceticism is simply a matter of following Jesus' core teaching, the essence of the kingdom of heaven — "love one another as I have loved you."

As we try to live this one simple statement, we know how poor in spirit we are. Loving those around us is a never-ending journey, one almost impossible to fulfill. We need to love our neighbors and even ourselves — and we have a lot of trouble coming close to this goal. Loving family, friends, strangers and enemies is a goal we seldom reach. We need divine help; we cannot do it by ourselves. We are beggars indeed.

In the end, facing death makes beggars of us all. As we come to death we enter a new dimension of reality. We may previously have had some experiences of the kingdom, but from the relative safety of physical existence and with at least some relation to life as we know it now. The final step of death, however, is very democratic, and it strips us of all our pretensions; it makes us truly poor and puts us on a level with all other human beings, even the poorest. Only the most brash and unthinking individuals can face death without some sense of impoverishment and fear. Perhaps the reason that Raymond Moody so seldom finds judgment in near-death experiences is that death makes us all beggars.

The Sorrowful and Gentle of Spirit

The natural reaction to facing one's beggarliness is to mourn. Sorrow is the normal emotional response to the pain and loss we feel when we cannot avoid our brokenness and helplessness. The reactions we call emotions involve the whole human being, *body* as well as mind and soul. Persons who truly mourn or grieve feel an inward heaviness, but that is not all. Their sorrow is also expressed outwardly in their downcast expression, and often in their tone of voice, in sighs and tears, and even in changes in the way their bodies function.

Many life situations can make us feel the emotion of sorrow. The most common is bereavement, grief over the loss of someone we love; we feel similar pain when we watch those we love suffer pain and illness. We also may grieve over loss of security or honor or position. Sometimes we are touched by the agony of other people, and we mourn because of the suffering so common in our broken world and because we can personally do so little to help; evil so often seems victorious. Our mourning can result from the compassion we feel as we think of the hungry, the mistreated, those who are dispossessed or imprisoned. When we have compassion, we suffer with and share in the pain of others; the root meaning of compassion is to suffer (*pati*) with (*cum*) another.

Some of us suffer inwardly as we look at how little we have accomplished in our lives. The different values within us often lay opposing claims upon us, and we find an inner warfare within us that keeps us from accomplishing our goals and from finding peace and harmony. Sometimes we are simply overwhelmed by a sense of inferiority and valuelessness. Or we may mourn because of the destructive and stupid actions we do not seem able to change. This attitude of sorrow and grief is very similar to an attitude of contrition and repentance. It is also our natural reaction as we become more completely aware of ourselves, our inner conflicts and problems and see how far we are from living in the kingdom.

According to Mark's Gospel Jesus began his public ministry with these words of incredibly good news: The time is fulfilled, and the kingdom of God has come near; repent, and believe the good news. (Mk 1:14) Jesus wanted people to see the glory of heaven that was bursting out around them. Once they recognized the magnificence of heaven they would then be filled with sorrow and repent because they were so far from it. Then they would strive to enter the fellowship of heaven.

This is the way of the sorrowful, whom Jesus called "blest" in the beatitudes. The sorrowful are those who mourn over their inner and outer poverty and allow the suffering to permeate their whole being, both physical and mental. When this sorrow permeates us, something happens: A new kind of life begins to emerge. When we really begin to feel sorrow over our inner condition and the tragedy of our world, we are born from above, and we become much more cautious about judging others. Repentance and mourning open the way to new life. And we can be born again and again; we can continually come to new spiritual insights and maturity.

Those who have never mourned have seldom been touched by the fullness of life. And those who go through life without experiencing love for other human beings may escape mourning; they may escape the devastating emotion that comes with any threat of losing our beloved, and they are usually protected from having to face themselves head-on. They pay a high price for this protection, however — isolation from the real world, a life without deep relationships with other human beings. Life on these terms is scarcely human. It is no wonder that such people are usually separated from the kingdom of heaven. They fail to develop the interdependence with and love of others that makes people fully human and fully alive. When we lose someone really close to us, our lives often collapse inside and we find that the kingdom of heaven is our greatest consolation.

Many people are afraid to let go and express their sorrow. The popular attitude in the Western world looks with distaste on expressions of grief; we are supposed to act like the captains of our souls at all times. When loss strikes, we are to bear up stoically, without making a fuss. We must never talk about the agony of death, of watching someone we have loved suffer and die. So any show of emotion, tears, or sobbing is to be avoided. Among men, tears are often seen as a sign of weakness, an almost unpardonable social disgrace, while the tears of women have been considered an evidence of their inferiority.

This is not the Christian attitude toward grief and mourning. It is rather the attitude of a world which fears looking at loss and pain because it doubts that there is any reality beyond them. The Christian knows that Abba and the kingdom are present to strengthen us and that it is healthy and honest to express our anguish through sorrow. From the Christian point of view it is both religiously and psychologically sound for people to show grief by breaking down in tears and sobs.

There is no reason to be ashamed of grief or of letting it be seen. At the tomb of Lazarus, Jesus unashamedly wept real tears, tears that welled up from a sorrowing heart. He also wept over Jerusalem when he saw how the people were bent on destruction. Mary, similarly, was weeping so hard at the grave of Jesus that she could not see through the veil of her tears and she failed to recognize her Lord when he appeared. David, too, shed tears of real anguish over his beloved Jonathan. He was apparently not ashamed of his feelings, since he set down the words of his magnificent expression of grief, which we still treasure (2 Sm 1:19-27). These were real men and women whom we remember for their gallant deeds as well as for their religious heroism. Unamuno once remarked that the chief sanctity of our temples is that they are places where men and women can come to weep together.

Tears and emotion are given to us for a purpose. They serve to release tension. They soothe the wounded heart, allowing the accumulation of pain to pour out so that it doesn't corrode the heart that bears it. Those who do not mourn generally do not find healing from their loss. Tears even contain an agent which destroys germs and helps protect us from disease. Many studies show evidence that unfaced grief may result in physical illness and be a contributing factor in the occurrence of cancer.

Grief is cured only as we pass through the center of it, through the opaque darkness of pain and anguish. It can't be circumvented or skirted without causing damage to the human psyche and keeping one far from the kingdom. We need to face our inner pain and let it bubble up. This does not mean giving way to ostentatious grief, but it does mean avoiding stoical repression.

Bearing real sorrow and grief gives one a larger heart, and this is essential if we are to minister to other people who are suffering grief from either inner or outer causes. Those who have passed through both kinds of sorrow and mourning and have found victory with the risen Christ can help others who face similar problems. In addition, passing through suffering provides an armor which strengthens us and gives us great power over calamity. Once we have faced grief and have survived, we are better able to stand whatever life brings.

Those who have passed through the vale of grief know the meaning of infinite resignation, that quality which Kierkegaard has described in these words:

> Infinite resignation is that shirt we read about in the old fable. The thread is spun under tears, the cloth bleached with tears, the shirt sewn with tears; but then too it is a better protection than iron and steel. The imperfection in the fable is that a third party can manufacture this shirt. The secret in life is that everyone must sew it for himself [sic], and the astonishing thing is that a man can sew it fully as well as a woman. In the infinite resignation there is peace and rest and comfort in sorrow — that is, if the movement is made normally.

Considering that grief apparently has such value, it is not surprising that Jesus calls those who mourn "blest" and says that they are given entrance into the kingdom.

This does not mean, of course, that there is no place in life for joy and carefree abandon and happiness. When one's whole being is absorbed by mourning and sadness and sorrow, there is little room for joy. We can distort life as much by avoiding joy and happiness as by ignoring suffering and grief. True living consists of both, and to ignore either our joy or our experiences of pain and loss can keep us from living in creative relation to the kingdom.

By clinging to the notion that life must be all one thing, either all good or all bad, we avoid the pulsating alternation, the virtual wavelike nature of human experience. It probably never occurred to Jesus that enough people would glorify sadness and grief to necessitate a warning against that idea. Such an attitude was rarely found in Jesus' time; it was developed by the Puritans and Jansenists, who perverted the meaning of Jesus' beatitude.

We should rejoice when life goes well, and a sense of being enlightened, creative, or prosperous gives reason for rejoicing. When there is reason for sorrow, either inner or outer, we need to mourn. But we must not allow these responses to keep us from sharing the feelings of others. Jesus told people to weep with those who weep and to rejoice with those who are rejoicing. When we are experiencing darkness, nothing is worse than to have a well-intentioned person suggest that something must be very wrong with us because we are showing so little joy. When we are truly rejoicing, it can be destructive to be met by a recital of all the frightful tragedies in this world.

Indeed, many times it is more difficult to find someone to laugh with us than to cry with us. We forget that making a creative adjustment to both the kingdom and our present life demands that we experience life's natural rhythms to the fullest. And this means that we must take the highs and lows when they come and not try to balance them out by feeling joy when we should be mourning, or the other way around.

We who have mourned are among those that are called the gentle or the meek. We have faced the pain in life and have picked up our lives and gone on. Mourning is our emotional response to poverty of spirit, while meekness is the kingdom's way of responding to grief and tragedy; we know the love of Christ is still near. We develop such meekness through facing the whole of life. Meekness is poverty of spirit in action: The meek or gentle are the unassuming, the humble, the considerate. They are not puffed up with pride or arrogance. They treat other people as equals, and they try to create the conditions that will allow others to develop to the maximum of their capacities. They are facilitators, listeners, who try to help others become what they are capable of becoming. They do not force their own goals onto others, not even onto husbands or wives, children or employees. In one French translation of the New Testament, the word *débonnaire* is used to translate "gentle" or "meek." It expresses this quality in a unique way. The meek are debonair about their lives. They take both the good and the bad equally well and go gently on, and they treat other people in the same way. These people live out Pauls description of love in 1 Corinthians 13: They are kindly, patient, and caring.

We sometimes confuse this virtue with the false and hypocritical humility portrayed so well in the character of Charles Dicken's Uriah Heep in *David Copperfield*. It is important, then, to remember that most virtues can be imitated through hypocrisy. La Rochefoucauld wrote that "hypocrisy is the homage which vice renders to virtue." A person with true gentleness of spirit can be distinguished by the way he or she accepts human beings as they are, without hopelessness. The finest example of this unassuming meekness is the way Jesus accepted arrest, mocking from religious leaders, false judgments, and torture on the cross. The quality of meekness touches a secret latch that opens the gate to heaven for anyone.

Seeking and the Kingdom

Gentleness, however, is not weakness. This quality of life results in true consideration for others and is more like the tough resilience of a reed growing by a stream. The reed bends with the wind and survives. Even a gale cannot uproot it, while the mighty oak may be torn from its roots and left to die. The meek or gentle can withstand lifes buffeting in a similar way. They develop a real inner strength. They listen to the deepest longings of their hearts and continue on, exerting themselves and seeking. They hunger and thirst after righteousness.

The Greek words for "hunger" and "thirst" have far more meaning than these words have in modern English. As I pored over the lexicons, the words' meanings came alive to me. *Hunger* and *thirst* speak of the human desire to reach out and achieve, to seek fulfillment of the deepest searching of the human heart. Love is essentially such a seeker. Love is that quality of life which is always reaching out, seeking to find the person who completes one's life and trying to find and complete the life of another person.

Even in the early Greek usage these words implied a need for more than just food and water. To hunger meant to need or desire something strongly, to crave it ardently. The hungry are those who are in need and who continue to seek; the word used in the beatitudes is also the one Luke used to warn the well-fed and satisfied that the time will come when they will need to hunger again (Lk 6:25). To thirst also indicated strong need or desire. When Jesus cried out from the cross "I thirst," this was the same word that he used to speak to the Samaritan woman about the living water that she could drink and never thirst again (Jn 19:28; 4:14-15).

Hunger and thirst were sometimes linked together by the Greeks to suggest the most extreme privation, the greatest need to seek fulfillment. In John's account of the feeding of the five thousand, Jesus spoke of bread from heaven and told the people, "I am the bread of life. Whoever comes to me shall never be hungry, and whoever believes in me shall never be thirsty" (Jn 6:35). Those of us who share in the bread of heaven will be given the fulfillment of the kingdom.

In the Book of Revelation, when John saw the first vision of the lamb on his throne, he was told that people who had gone through their ordeal and come to the Lamb would never again feel hunger or thirst

(Rv 7:16). Likewise, the early Church was convinced that those who know their need are candidates for heaven and that in the kingdom they will find a relationship with Christ which will meet their deepest needs. The hungry and thirsty, the church realized, are more open to the kingdom than people who are seeking to be filled largely by power, money, and things. Those whose wants are already satisfied are seldom pushed to keep on seeking. They lose sight of the kingdom and the joy they might find in it. In Goethe's *Faust*, as the angels come to rescue Faust from the Evil One, they sing, "Those whose seeking never ceases are ours for their redeeming." Heaven loves seekers even if they have sought the wrong things.

What does it mean, then, to hunger and thirst *for righteousness*? There are few words in the New Testament that have been discussed so thoroughly. The New Testament makes it very clear that there is more to righteousness than just moral and legal right thinking and acting. Paul suggested that people do not become righteous simply by following the law, but rather by accepting God's grace and mercy humbly, with meekness. Whatever the God of love approves becomes the ultimate righteousness. We become righteous by relentless seeking for the kingdom and then by sharing the love we have experienced in the kingdom with others. As we hunger and thirst for true satisfaction, we experience the incredible loving presence of God, and we lose it if we do not share it with other men, women, and children.

Persistent seekers, Jesus emphasized, are on their way to the kingdom of heaven. In the Sermon on the

Mount, Jesus also told his listeners, "Set your mind on God's kingdom and his justice before everything else, and all the rest will come to you as well" (Mt 6:33, NEB; Lk 12:31). And he further instructed them, "Ask, and you will receive; seek, and you will find, knock, and the door will be opened" (Mt 7:7; Lk 11:9, NEB). We who ask and seek and knock do find that doors are opened; we receive our requests and we find our treasure. We touch the reality of the kingdom now, and hence we want to share with others spiritually and materially.

Jesus told two characteristic stories to emphasize our constant need for seeking Abba's presence, even if we appear to be nagging the Holy One. Both stories suggest that Abba likes to be pestered by human beings about their needs. The first is the parable of the obstinate widow, who pestered the judge until she was given justice, and the second tells about the man who got a neighbor out of bed in the middle of the night to borrow some bread (Lk 18:1-7; 11:5-9). The Creator is a loving Abba, but the Holy One does not pamper us. God wants us to seek the holy persistently, patiently, consistently. It is not enough to just ask once and then assume our request will be granted. It takes persistent prayer to open the door to the kingdom. Such persistence is important because it shows that we are seeking the Divine's presence consistently, again and again. Receiving Abba's presence is more important than any specific gift; we receive the fellowship of heaven.

Deep within us there is something vital and searching, something restless, that sends us on strange quests and keeps us searching for deeper and deeper meaning. If we have not stifled it, there is within each of us an insatiable thirst for something that will be truly satisfying. Augustine suggested that God placed within us a hunger which only the Divine can satisfy so that we must seek the Holy One again and again in order to be satisfied. If we follow our inner hunger and thirst and do not give up, we are led inevitably and unerringly to heaven both now and for eternity. We may be led through strange and difficult places, but in the end we arrive. Abba made us restless so we might find our rest in eternal Love.

One can observe this hunger and thirst in normal children as they start out to explore and understand the world. Nothing has to be done to develop an inquisitive, seeking spirit in children. All that we need to do is to release their adventuring thirst. The trouble with so much of our educational process is that it turns this torrent of desire and interest into a barely observable trickle. The average child is naturally a seeker before ever attending school; however, most schools and many parents suppress this questing spirit with their rigidity and rules and prohibitions and tedium. Few of us ever come to our full stature as adults because this spirit of childlike seeking is one of the elements of full adulthood and is difficult to regain once it is lost. Such childlike seeking is an essential quality of the kingdom of heaven.

The source of our seeking is the reality, energy, or substance that we call love. Love is the mainspring, the source of all our searching, particularly of our search for meaning. Few people have described the vital importance of love better than Carl Jung in his autobiography, which he wrote near the end of his life:

In my medical experience as well as in my own life I have again and again been faced with the mystery of love, and have never been able to explain what it is. . . . Whatever one can say, no words express the whole. To speak of partial aspects is always too much or too little, for only the whole is meaningful. Love "bears all things" and "endures all things" (1 Cor 13:7). These words say all there is to be said; nothing can be added to them. For we are in the deepest sense the victims and the instruments of cosmogonic "love. . . ." Being a part, man cannot grasp the whole. He is at its mercy. He may assent to it, or rebel against it; but he is always caught up by it and enclosed within it. He is dependent upon it and is sustained by it. Love is his light and his darkness, whose end he cannot see."Love ceases not" — whether he speaks with the "tongues of angels," or with scientific exactitude traces the life of the cell down to its uttermost source.

Jung concludes his description of love by stating that the words "love" and "God" refer to the same reality.

Laurens van der Post has also pointed out this seeking power of love, its power to lead or even force us toward one another and toward new life. In his novel *The Face Beside the Fire*, van der Post writes:

When the world and judgment say: "This is the end," love alone can see the way out. It is the aboriginal tracker, the African bushman

on the faded desert spoor within us, and its
unfailing quarry is always the light.

If we want to find God and the holy fellowship of
heaven, the surest way is to listen to the depth of
ourselves and discover this insatiable desire that leads
us to find the Holy One, and to share the divine love
with other human beings whose need for us is the
greatest.

Over the years I have known many people in depth.
I have found this restless search for love in every one
of them, even the most distorted or depraved. There
have been none who did not, in the depth of their
being, seek for more love than they felt life, as they
knew it, could offer. Hunger and thirst are deep
within us and more persistent than most of us realize.
They help us dream the impossible dream.

Once again we need to recognize that love is not
just our *feeling* of love for others but consists of our
actions of love to our neighbors, inspired by the love
we have received from Abba. Both feeling and action
are necessary. Without divine love pouring into us,
we go dry. Without love for other human beings, we
can slowly cut ourselves off from the sustaining flow
of love from Abba.

What truly counts in our lives is not so much what
we actually accomplish; it is more important to strive
— to keep on seeking, trusting that somehow, some-
where, the dream of complete fulfillment and relationship will come true. The Holy One does not seem
to reject people who seek in the wrong direction. The
only ones who may find the door to the kingdom
closed and locked are the lukewarm, those who will

not leave the fireside and go out searching. The experience that turned Paul's life around is a case in point. Paul was *seeking* when it happened. Although he was seeking in the wrong direction — supporting the high priests in their efforts to put Christianity out of business — his seeking led him straight into the presence of the Christ on the Damascus road. This experience started Paul out on a totally new life. He became the apostle of love, proclaiming the mercy of Abba and the need for human beings to love one another and have mercy on all people.

The Merciful and the Pure in Heart

Most of us find it difficult to be merciful. Mercy means forgiveness, and it is not easy for us to forgive those who hurt us or who we think have hurt us. We each have some pet anger, resentment, grudge, or bitterness that we hang onto even though we realize that there are real rewards for being merciful and forgiving. Actually, it is downright foolish to nurse anger and bitterness; as John Sanford has remarked, feeding the fires of anger and resentment simply ties us more and more firmly to the very people from whom we wish to be free.

Jesus was clear about the importance of mercy and forgiveness. In the Lord's Prayer he included only one condition: We can expect God to give freely all that we need, including forgiveness, so long as we are able to forgive other human beings. People who cannot offer such mercy to others are caught by dark forces that corrupt and destroy. When we will not forgive, we allow our vengeance and anger to possess us. We are no longer masters in our own homes; we let anger, pride, and self-justification take charge. We then shut out the kingdom of heaven, which is seeking to give us all its gifts.

What do I need to forgive? Sometimes in saying the Lord's Prayer I simply say: *Forgive us our unconsciousness (our lack of awareness), as we forgive the unconsciousness of others.* When we are unaware or unconscious, we forget who we are and what we are doing; we then say cruel things and perform cruel deeds. In his book, *The Forgiveness of Sins*, Charles Williams' notes that there are things which need not be forgiven, things which ought to be forgiven, and things which cannot be forgiven — and the Christian forgives them all.

Williams knew from experience what he was sharing with his readers. At the time he was writing, the Germans were bombing London, and Williams realized that those unleashing this terror were caught up unconsciously in the darkness of Hitler. Like so many of us in our ordinary lives, the Germans were reacting to unconscious forces bent on destruction; nonetheless, Williams understood that Christians are called to forgive even the Nazis. Much the same understanding is found among the early Christians. When Saint Perpetua, for instance, was about to be thrown to the wild beasts in the arena, a guard asked her why she did not curse her jailers. She told him that they were already under the power of darkness and she did not wish to add to it by curses or condemnation. Mercy and compassion are essential if we are to participate fully in the kingdom of God, both now and eternally.

The next question is a little harder to answer. How can I achieve this important quality of life, this spirit of forgiveness? I cannot become forgiving by an act of will alone. I can consciously decide, "I am going to show mercy to everyone." But then, just when I'm in the midst of some difficulty, someone with an irritating manner walks into the room; a biting remark slips out of my mouth and the person goes away hurt. Or I may be simply angry about where life has placed me, and I am nasty for no reason at all to the first person I meet. Or I may join in an ugly gossip session, not realizing that the person I condemn really needs my compassion and forgiveness. There can even be times when life seems so burdensome that I turn my back on other people's troubles and do not reach out a hand or give them the "kiss of peace" they need.

But Jesus placed no limits on how many times we need to forgive and have mercy. When Peter asked his master if he should forgive seven times, Jesus replied: "Not seven times, but, I tell you, seventy times seven" — in other words, indefinitely (Mt 18:21-22). But how can we imperfect human beings ever achieve this level of mercy and forgiveness? I have struggled with this question for forty-five years.

First of all, we have to take Jesus seriously and make the decision to try to let forgiveness and mercy rule our lives.

Second, we need to keep some record of our failures and successes. It is difficult to perceive the direction of our lives unless we keep a notebook or journal of our moral and spiritual progress.

Third, when an individual annoys us without any particular reason, we need to look at our own faults and see what buried secrets in our own lives have triggered our reaction.

Fourth, if we are to forgive anyone, we need to resolve *never* to strike out physically or materially to harm the person who we think has offended us.

Fifth, we must never say anything ugly or catty about anyone. Bridling the tongue takes infinite care. This suggestion is particularly difficult when others have started a moral dissection of one we do not like.

Sixth, we should pray regularly for the person who seems unworthy of our mercy. Gossiping about or hurting one whom we have asked the divine Lover to care for or protect puts us in a ridiculous position.

Seventh, we can begin to look for some positive quality in the person toward whom we wish to show mercy. When a group of people is bent on tearing down a person's character, one positive observation from us can often change the whole atmosphere. Most gossip is notably unmerciful.

Eighth, performing some act of kindness for one who has hurt us can change our attitude. We love our children so much not because they act thoughtfully toward us but because we have done so much for them.

Of course, we must keep on trying consciously to show mercy, directing our hearts and minds to follow through as far as we can. We also need to reflect on the times when we have failed to be merciful, and then we must try to see how we can change. However, as I've already mentioned, our conscious determination is not enough. Mercy is part of a way of life; it flows naturally from a life marked by poverty of spirit. Those who truly mourn seldom spend time pointing out other people's faults. There is no better evidence of gentleness of spirit than a forgiving and merciful attitude. Those who are seeking usually know how difficult it is to find their goal, their treasure, "the pearl of great price," and they are not likely to blame anyone else who falls short or gets lost in the search. Mercy wells up out of a childlike spirit. It would be good for us all to pray the ancient prayer: Abba, in your unbounded mercy, you have revealed the beauty of your power through your constant forgiveness of our sins. The power of this love be in our hearts to bring your pardon and your kingdom to all we meet.

People who live in glass houses — as all of us really do — are wise not to throw stones. I am just as vulnerable as the person I might be preparing to attack or find fault with. Once we realize that we are all beggars in the spirit, unable to achieve our goals and yet continuing to seek, we know that none of us is in any position to judge any other person. If we judge and are not merciful, we are not living in the kingdom. We are not acting as beggars in spirit. Lacking mercy for others, we remain blind to the planks in our own eyes and avoid the effort of searching for purity of heart. Such a path does not prepare us for the kingdom.

In his book, *Purity of Heart,* Kierkegaard suggests that the pure in heart are those whose wills are directed toward one goal. They act from one central motive, one center of being. They become one person, as the many selves within them are joined together in seeking one common purpose. Like everyone else, I have many selves within me. As one or another of them comes to the fore, my personality changes.

None of us are simple, unitary souls. I have described the complexity of the human spirit at some length in my book *Discernment: A Study in Ecstasy and Evil.* Within each of us, there are many different powers and voices, many different desires struggling for control. Our task, as followers of Christ, is to try to bring this menagerie together into one, undivided personality. This seldom happens to any of us until we realize our poverty of spirit and try to face all aspects of our being, asking that they be brought together into harmony by an act of grace.

The Greek words for "pure in heart" used in Jesus' beatitude are very revealing. We have a tendency to think of the heart largely in medical or very materialistic terms. We do not often speak of heart as an intangible part of our human reality. In Greek, the heart was understood to mean only secondarily a physical organ; however, it was first of all considered the center and source of our inner life. The heart was the source of all that makes a human being — thinking, playing, feeling, loving, willing. It was the organ of natural and spiritual enlightenment, as well as the center of our passions and desires. "Heart" stood for the life within human beings on all fronts from physical and mental to moral and spiritual. In our materialistic time it is difficult to realize that the *psyche* or the soul was as real to the Greeks as the physical body is to us.

Katharós, or "pure" in Greek, is a word rich with nuances of meaning. It was used to speak of substances — especially water or metals — that are clear, clean, free of admixture. The word also could describe feelings that are unmixed, or a way that is open and clear, or something sound and undamaged. It also meant ceremonially and morally clean, free from offense or contamination. The person who was described as *katharós* in heart was sincere and single-minded, innocent, guiltless, blameless. Pure-hearted individuals have taken the trouble to learn about what is in the depth of their being. They seek to act as simple, unified beings, rather than as noisy mixtures of fragmented and scattered parts. Christians of this kind are trying to follow the teachings that Jesus gave about singleness of purpose and purity of heart.

In his parable comparing the eye to a lamp, Jesus taught that having a single eye, a sound eye, will give light to the whole body. And he went on to say that no one can serve two masters (Mt 6:22-24). He warned that every kingdom divided against itself is headed for ruin and collapse, and that if the house of the soul is divided against itself, it cannot stand (Mt 12:25). Only a good tree, Jesus said, can bear good fruit, and a bad or corrupt tree will always be known by its bad fruit (Mt 12:33). Jesus ridiculed the Pharisees for their concern about ritual cleanliness. He explained to the disciples that humans are not defiled by what goes into the body, but by the evil that comes out of the mouth and proceeds from the heart — and then he gives a list of such evils: "evil intentions, murder, adultery, fornication, theft, false witness, slander" (Mt 15:1-20).

But purity of heart, like mercy and forgiveness, cannot be achieved solely by our own will and effort. It is a gift that is given to individuals who recognize their poverty and work at filling themselves from the one source which can satisfy the hunger and thirst of our souls. And our preparation to receive this gift is not exactly easy. John Sanford points out very clearly in *The Kingdom Within* that the purity Jesus was talking about does not originate alone from outer actions. Real purity of heart comes to those who are growing in knowledge and acceptance of themselves and those around them. The light of the kingdom begins to shine through every part of their being and brings love to those around them. For most of us, this requires a whole new attitude.

When people take this way of single-mindedness, they come to know poverty of spirit and mourning. They find the meaning of mercy and gentleness of spirit and they realize the need to keep on seeking. It is comforting to realize that the beggars in spirit are given an equal place in the kingdom beside the pure of heart. True purity of heart is more an attitude than a condition or state of life. It is the attitude which makes us willing to know ourselves, and to work at bringing each aspect of ourselves into harmonious relation with the kingdom and its goals. Blessed indeed are the single-minded, those with a single eye; they shall behold the Holy One in a kingdom that is drawing near now and is totally fulfilled in eternity.

The Peacemakers and the Persecuted

People who bring mercy into concrete reality by creating harmony and peace among men and women are known as peacemakers. The Greek word for peace is *eírënë*, from which we get the name Irene and also "irenic," or that which is conducive to peace, harmony, moderation, and conciliation. The Hebrew word *shalom* expresses much the same meaning. It describes a state of peace in which we are free from both inner and outer strife and war; we live in harmony and health. A peaceful life is well-ordered, secure, and prosperous. This state of peace and contentment with life comes to people who have experienced God's love and the fellowship of heaven. They then feel impelled to share harmony and love, joy and peace with and among all people.

In the Lord's Prayer we ask for Abba's will to be done and the kingdom to come on earth as it is in heaven. The peacemakers are those who are trying to bring this about. They are instruments of the kingdom, who encourage people to taste this state of harmony in which all people work together in joy and peace. *The Divine Comedy*, Dante's superb portrayal of paradise, gives a picture of this state. Dante depicts paradise as a place in which each person abides in a situation which suits that individual best, and yet each one shares in the total peace, love, and joy found by all the others in heaven.

This state is not found often on earth, because we find so much disharmony, war, strife, hatred, poverty, and want among human beings. The peacemakers look out over the earth and see the world as it is; they cannot escape becoming beggars in spirit. They know little has been accomplished by their own efforts, but *they do not give up*. They continue their effort to help our broken societies realize the peace of God's kingdom. This is probably why they are called children of God: As peacemakers, they share in the very nature of the Holy One, who came among us at Christmas to bring peace and joy. Continually growing in peace within themselves, they humbly seek to share the kingdom with others. Those who have little peace within themselves can do little to help bring peace and harmony to others.

Martin Luther King was one of the great peacemakers of our time. He knew himself; he knew his own anger and hatred. After being reviled or thrown into jail, he had to quiet down and bring his own inner violence to the Christ and allow peace to return to his soul. The greatest of all peacemakers, of course, was Jesus, and especially during the last days of his life Jesus became the symbol and model of peacemaking. He took on himself the angers and hatred of the world and turned them into peace. As human peacemakers, we face and carry the burden of our own imperfections and poverty and share with others whatever peace we find. The first requirement for peacemakers is a sincere desire to share the fine wine of the kingdom with all who would taste it. And the second requirement is for them to know their own motives well enough to be certain that they do not offer peace with one hand and show a clenched fist with the other.

Unless I know myself well, I am always in danger of trying to promote good for violent reasons. Several years ago at the University of Notre Dame, I was a member of a team who designed a series of courses to study the use of non-violence in bringing peace to society and the world. It soon became clear, however, that the students who enrolled in these courses often had violent motives for undertaking non-violence. So we then added courses on personal perspectives in non-violence. As we examined our own reactions within these groups, we learned how much violence each of us has within us and how fearful we are of one another. We cannot hope to bring peace to other people in this troubled world until we know ourselves well and recognize the violence within us that is ready to boil over each time we are upset. We need to realize, again, our poverty of spirit and how much help we need to handle these destructive urges.

As I have listened to people trying to unscramble their lives, again and again I have been faced with the truth that most people want to love. This means that they want to be peacemakers, for those who love are peacemakers. But most of us are afraid. We are afraid that if we let the power and peace of the kingdom really flow through us, the world will pass us by or we will be ground under its heel. We are afraid to give up our anxious, angry, bitter, cantankerous selves and become instruments of peace. It is so easy, we feel, to be deluded and to make mistakes.

We forget that great peacemakers like Francis of Assisi made mistakes and did not give up. Few individuals have done as much as Francis to show Christians the way of peace. Yet even he could be deceived. He preached the Children's Crusade in which tens of thousands of innocent children were killed or made slaves. Thus, even the greatest peacemakers are not perfect. If we want peace for ourselves and others, we have to take the risk of trying, perhaps failing, perhaps making mistakes, and then trying again. We can hardly do better than to follow the way described by Francis in these words:

Lord,
make me an instrument of your peace.
Where there is hatred, let me sow love;
where there is doubt, faith;
where there is despair, hope;
where there is darkness, light;
and where there is sadness, joy.

O Divine Master,
grant that I may not so much seek
to be consoled as to console,
to be understood as to understand,
to be loved as to love.

For it is in giving that we receive,
it is in pardoning that we are pardoned,
and it is in dying that we are born to eternal
life.

Obviously we cannot follow this way if we put our own desire for peace, consolation, and love ahead of the needs of others. To become peacemakers we have to try the way of unselfishness and love, and to aim at more than achieving peace just for ourselves. Even when our efforts are not very successful, they can bring us closer to the kingdom of heaven by making us appreciate the value of peace and the danger of violence.

Honesty and sensitivity are essential qualities of the peacemaker. To find peace means being reconciled first with our human situation just as it is. Most of us would rather be lulled into a false sense of security by ignoring the less pleasant aspects of our human condition. In Charles Williams' poetry about King Arthur and the knights of the Round Table, William's pictures Galahad asking his father Lancelot to pardon him for being such a pure individual, knowing that Lancelot must find his son's purity hard to bear. In this portrayal, Williams suggests that Galahad accepts the flawed human condition — he understands his father's humanness. We need this kind of sensitivity and honesty to start on the road toward peace.

These first seven qualities that Jesus calls blessed in the beatitudes prepare us for the kingdom. However, they do not always bring appreciation and admiration from the religious or secular world. Jesus did not offer us false promises that the kingdom way would be easy. Peacemakers often make angry and violent people angrier and more violent and so they often strike back in anger and persecute the peacemakers. In addition, those who are really trying to follow the way laid out by Christ are usually condemned whenever that way conflicts with the ideas and rules of our secular society. Jesus concludes with an eighth beatitude: How blest are those who have suffered persecution for the cause of right; the kingdom of heaven is theirs.

Jesus used strong words to speak of the persecution that is suffered for the sake of righteousness. He spoke of insults and every kind of lie, comparing it to the violent treatment of the prophets in former times. Followers of Christ have often been persecuted, harassed, mistreated, pushed out of the way, put to flight, pursued, and even killed. They have been reviled and upbraided, insulted and shamed. Individuals who are treated in this way have no choice but to bear their crosses if they wish to go on following Christ. They cannot say that they did not know what they were getting into. Jesus warned that following him might lead to opposition, calumny and persecution. While the manners of society have become somewhat more polite in our time (with some notable exceptions), the world still has ways of showing its contempt for people who show a need for much more than conventional religion. To bear persecution requires the divine gift of courage.

The suffering that can come from persecution opens an immediate door into Abba's kingdom. But this does not mean that we can find that doorway by *inviting* persecution, seeking it out either consciously or unconsciously. Persecution suffered for the cause of right is one thing. Any other kind is a form of self-destructiveness which the early Church took care to condemn. Efforts to seek martyrdom have always been considered a sign of sickness, not of holiness. Real Christianity still makes clear that mistreating oneself or needlessly exposing oneself to persecution does not lead to the kingdom. Violence against ourselves and self-condemnation can cut us off from the kingdom of heaven just as effectively as striking others violently.

We need, therefore, to be peacemakers within ourselves as well as in the outer world. Violence against ourselves is destructive. In his challenging book, *Man Against Himself*, Karl Menninger has described the many complex ways in which we can turn our human self-destructiveness upon our bodies and minds and damage them. We need to be very aware of this in order to avoid self-persecution, which leads away from the kingdom, and yet be willing to bear the pain of unavoidable persecution. We must be aware that violence, whether turned upon oneself or others, usually comes from evil.

Courage is necessary if we are to bear the persecution the world inflicts on us for trying to follow the way of Jesus. The way of the kingdom has never been very popular in this secular world. Prophets are often misunderstood and harassed. Those who are persecuted can do no better than to follow the example of Jesus, who gracefully bore persecution in the days just before his crucifixion and resurrection. The way of the cross is a way of courage as well as of meekness. I doubt if anyone who does not have courage can maintain a truly humble attitude. Meekness that is not reinforced by courage can become weakness and sentimentality. In the beatitudes, Jesus gave us fair warning that he was not offering an easy way, and he demonstrated the kind of courage that is required when he went up to Jerusalem to confront the powers of darkness. I have described this courage in my book *The Cross*, which deals with the universal meaning of Jesus' crucifixion.

A doorway of couragous bearing of persecution opens into the kingdom. Those who may not be able to enter by way of peacemaking, humility or even mourning can go in through this door. In his poetic vision, Dante saw various circles of heaven, each appropriate for a different virtue. There was a special place for warriors of the spirit, for the courageous and the brave who were persecuted.

It must be remembered, however, that courage is virtuous only if it is tied to persecution for the cause of right. It is foolhardy rather than courageous to court persecution needlessly or for an evil or vengeful reason. Such actions do not bring us closer to the kingdom, but take us in the wrong direction — although, if foolhardy actions are the result of our being misguided or misinformed, our good intentions are taken into account.

I am very glad that bearing persecution is only one of eight doors into the kingdom of heaven.

Finding the Kingdom

Luke's account of the beatitudes includes a warning about the way that leads away from the kingdom (Lk 6:20-26). The rich, Jesus warned, have had their time of happiness. Those who have been stuffed full will go hungry. Those who see none of the tragedy in the world and who laugh now will mourn and weep hereafter. People who are admired, those of whom everyone speaks well, may be like false prophets. Obviously Jesus felt that certain things should be avoided if people are to find their way into the kingdom.

Self-satisfaction and pride in what we have and what we are can keep us tied to the values and short-lived satisfactions of this world. Pride can make us overbearing and keep us from knowing ourselves. We end up judging others rather than stopping to realize that there is a listener within who sees us as we truly are. We can remain split so that purity of mind and singleness of heart are impossible for us. The world often thinks highly of us, and yet we may be losing our lives we think we have gained. Also to be avoided is the careless attitude that leads people to go along with whatever the world offers. Since such people lack the seriousness to keep at a search, life usually leads them on a broad road away from the kingdom.

Some people, it is true, get their fill of living like this. They come to mourn their senseless boredom and begin to seek, and I am sure that it is *never too late for anyone* who honestly asks Abba to show him or her the way to the kingdom. But our task as Christians is to be ready to point the way by our examples. Our first job is to realize our own need. Then we must try to do our best to make silence, prayer, faith, love, service, and peace central in our lives.

Outside of the beatitudes, the most specific direction that Jesus gave us about finding the kingdom of heaven was his instruction that the best way is to become like little children. Children, in their truly natural state, show most of the virtues which Jesus named as qualifications for the kingdom. Except for the few who have been abused or ignored by adults, children are humble and self-effacing, poor in spirit. They can experience and express their fears and joys. Children are easily touched by love and they share love with others. Because their inner and outer natures are in almost complete accord, they are single-minded and guileless. They are naturally direct, honest, and unassuming.

Children also have a natural passion to learn and to grow. They are striving to become, to fulfill what is in them. Few things are so sad as a child whose growth has been arrested. Real-life Peter Pans are not often very attractive; this is *not* what Jesus meant when he said that we must become like children. In addition, most children are merciful and have a desire to bring harmony and peace to parents and to those they love. Adults do not very often realize how easily a child loses this spirit and learns another way from adults and other children who are disagreeable and angry, some of them abusive. Most violent children have been abused; some children are like lambs led to slaughter and some are abandoned. But the child — the real child, by nature, before being pummeled into grown-up shapes and postures — is the model of growing and becoming, and so is a model of the qualities that lead into the kingdom. Growth and becoming are the key words. This is the pattern that Jesus gave us to follow. When we cease to develop in this way, we step into the rigidity of self-satisfied adulthood. The kingdom is so complete and perfect, and we human beings so imperfect and incomplete, that all of us who feel we have already achieved our full potential have missed the basic message of eternal growth and development which makes the kingdom everlastingly attractive.

What is heaven like? Heaven is the incredible fellowship of all the unassuming, recovering people who are being consoled and strengthened. They are kind and patient, creative and merciful. All of them are filled with divine love and wish to help us become Abba's peacemaking children so that we too may fully live out our ever expanding, eternal divine destiny with joy.

How can we ask for anything more than what the fellowship of God's kingdom provides for us now and forever?

For Further Reading

In my book *Afterlife: The Other Side of Dying* (Mahwah, New Jersey: Paulist Press, 1979; New York: Crossroad, 1982) I provide an overview of the entire subject of the Christian view of eternal life. In addition to describing Jesus view of heaven, I give a theological foundation for the Christian view, an analysis of human experiences of eternal life, and a description of Dantes superb poem on afterlife, *The Divine Comedy*. I also deal with the idea of reincarnation, the problem of hell, and a method of ministering to the dying. A comprehensive bibliography on the subject is added.

An excellent edition of Dante's great work, with enough notes to help us understand it, is found in Dante (Alighieri), *The Divine Comedy*, translated by Dorothy L. Sayers and Barbara Reynolds, Baltimore: Penguin Books. Vol. I: *Hell*, 1949. Vol. II: *Purgatory*, 1955. Vol. III: *Paradise*, 1962. An excellent illustrated introduction to Dante's great work was written by Helen Luke *Dark Wood to White Rose* (New York: Parabola Books, 1989).

Martin Israel, a medical doctor and a profound Christian writer, has published his reflections on the subject in: *Life Eternal*, Cambridge, MA: Cowley Publications, 1993.

John A. Sanford gives a profound analysis of the kingdom parables in *The Kingdom Within,* San Francisco: Harper Collins, 1990. He also provides the definitive study of reincarnation within the Christian Church: *Soul Journey: A Jungian Analyst Looks at Reincarnation*, New York: Crossroad, 1991. Franz Riklin, former president of the Institute of Jungian Analysts in Zürich, Switzerland, has written an excellent unpublished paper, *Psychotherapy and Death* in which dreams of dying people present the same data as near-death experiences. I hope to publish this article in the future. Dr. Riklin concludes his study stating that the human psyche does not view death as the end of conscious life.

Few theologians deal with the subject of religious experience that can give us a taste of heaven now. I have dealt with the importance of religious experience in: *Companions on the Inner Way: The Art of Spiritual Guidance*, New York: Crossroad, 1983 as well as in *The Other Side of Silence*, Mahwah NJ: Paulist Press, 1995.

Meeting the risen Christ in vision or dream certainly gives us an intimation of heaven. Henri Nouwen describes his experience in *Beyond the Mirror: Reflections on Death and Life*, New York: Crossroad, 1990. G. Scott Sparrow has been aware of such experiences, and he has recorded scores of these experiences that have been healing and consoling to those who received them. I wrote an introduction for Sparrow's excellent book, *I Am with You Always: True Stories of Encounters with Jesus*, New York: Bantam, 1995.

Raymond Moody, Jr. wrote his popular book *Life after Life*, New York: Bantam, 1976, without declaring what he believed. However, in his book *The Light Beyond*, New York: Bantam, 1986, Moody drops his scientific objectivity and says that he believes that near death experiences do give us a glimpse of heaven.

Outside the Christian community there is wide interest in what experience we can have of heaven or eternal life. In a book edited by Gary Doore — *What Survives: Contemporary Explorations of Life after Death*, Los Angeles: Tarcher, 1990 —there is no mention of any Christian view of eternal life! From a Buddhist point of view, only the eternal is real. We prepare ourselves for real life by detaching ourselves from all earthly attachments. This point of view along with real wisdom about treating the dying, is found in: Stephen Levine, *Who Dies? An Investigation of Conscious Living and Conscious Dying*, New York: Bantam Doubleday Dell, An Anchor Book, 1982.

HOW TO READ THE GOSPELS
Answers to Common Questions
by **Daniel Harrington, S.J.**

In a straightforward and unassuming way, Harrington offers a delightful instruction into the deeper realities of the Gospels.

"Harrington's introduction to the Gospels is excellent. Written on a popular level, with all technical terminology well explained."

Joseph A. Fitzmyer, S.J.
Catholic University of America

ISBN 1-56548-076-7
paperback, 51/8 x 8, 96 pp., $6.95

And . . .

OUR AGE
The Historic New Era of Christian-Jewish Understanding
by **Rabbis Jack Bemporad and Michael Shevack**
Foreword by **John Cardinal O'Connor**

Our Age focuses on the dramatic historical change in Jewish-Christian understanding. It offers vital insights into how Christians and Jews can build true and healthy relationships in the fast-paced world of today.

"As honest and even-handed a treatment of Jewish-Christian relations as I have ever read . . . I am deeply grateful for Our Age."

John Cardinal O'Connor
Archbishop of New York

ISBN 1-56548-081-3
paperback, 51/8 x 8, 96 pp., $6.95

To order phone 1- 800 - 462-5980